MW01028171

Contemplative Provocations

FR. DONALD HAGGERTY

Contemplative Provocations

IGNATIUS PRESS   SAN FRANCISCO

Cover photograph by Elia Kahvedjian
Jerusalem

Cover design by Roxanne Mei Lum

© 2013 by Ignatius Press, San Francisco
All rights reserved
ISBN 978-1-58617-733-1
Library of Congress Control Number 2012942821
Printed in the United States of America ∞

To my mother and father

Contents

Foreword

The very title of this work by Fr. Donald Haggerty, *Contemplative Provocations*, describes something of the author's methodology and the achievable purpose he envisions for anyone who would read this rich manuscript. This is truly a thought-provoking effort, offering what appears to be a kind of "manual of personal cooperation with the grace of God" and some spiritual direction. In much the same way as Saint Ignatius' great classic, the *Spiritual Exercises*, might be thought of as a type of manual on how to direct a week or month of retreat on the spiritual pilgrimage of life, Fr. Haggerty's work might indeed be read as a road map for the ambitious migration of the spiritual life through the darkness and emptiness of the "mission of charity" as lived by Blessed Mother Teresa of Calcutta, and carried on by her Missionaries of Charity. Fidelity to this pilgrimage leads toward the light and fulfillment of the desert spiritually transformed.

This is not a "do-it-yourself kit" but rather, it is an honest effort to extend spiritual advancement in the courageous pilgrimage of faith to all walks of life and to explain the terms of that advancement more practically, profoundly, and invitingly. This is not some peace-filled, undisturbed vision, some comfortable distance away from the challenging field of the spiritual combat for real growth; this is no idyllic view from a restful hillside or shore. This offers a battle plan, a tactical set of suggestions for the "road less traveled".

Contemplative Provocations teaches us that faith grows in the Church by contemplation, study, lived experience and obedience to the Magisterium, a formula suggested by the Second Vatican Council for the whole Church. It provides an experiential guide, a truly inductive approach to time-proven methods, based strongly on Eucharistic reflections nourished by the Word of God (*the very words of Christ*) in the practice and interpretation of the Church. This is a shared experience of one who is truly trying to work out his own spirituality as a priest, and many of his insights are most inspiring. This work presents the vocation of the baptized as a search for absolute, authentic holiness, an effort to live by the gift of wisdom, judging reality by its ultimate causes, that one reality which is necessary. The text is based solidly on the tradition of the Church, as is clear from even a cursory glance at the chapter headings:

"Faith's Passion." "Faith's Blindness." "The Mind in Prayer." "Poverty of Soul."

I find that three features stand out in Fr. Haggerty's work:

1. The author offers a genuine insight into *kenosis*: a "putting on the mind of Christ Jesus" (cf. Phil 2:5ff.): there is presented here a real possibility of living a life in Christ, a life in the Holy Spirit (see CCC 1691ff.).

2. These pages do not presume to indoctrinate or give precise solutions for overcoming the usual struggles in prayer. Rather, they offer a hope that the faithful believer who strives to live more and more in correspondence with God's grace will develop an interior longing. We need a deeper receptivity. A lifelong living of the *fiat* of Christian Baptism makes us more aware of the disproportion within ourselves.

3. This is more like a modern approach to the ministry of encouragement, a kind of modern *paranesis*, or *paraclesis*, inspired by the Paraclete, in which all the baptized are moved to help one another along the way of the Cross: "Joseph who was surnamed by the apostles Barnabas (which means, Son of encouragement)" (Acts 4:36).

The author makes a strong appeal also for personal study:

Catholic doctrinal truth and sound spirituality are companions. They support and protect each other; they shed luminosity on the importance of the other. But they also starve together when either is neglected, when one does not nourish the other.

This paragraph is so reminiscent of the beautiful ideal expressed in the *Catechism of the Catholic Church*:

> In the work of teaching and applying Christian morality, the Church needs the dedication of pastors, the knowledge of theologians, and the contribution of all Christians and men of good will. Faith and the practice of the Gospel provide each person with an experience of life "in Christ," who enlightens him and makes him able to evaluate the divine and human realities according to the Spirit of God. Thus the Holy Spirit can use the humblest to enlighten the learned and those in the highest positions. (CCC 2038)

Fr. Haggerty's experience with Mother Teresa's "darkness" as well as the "dark night" of Saint John of the Cross have enabled the author to see farther in the darkness:

> A larger number of these thoughts have some link to my contact with Mother Teresa's Missionaries of Charity. Many observations on these pages had a beginning in conversations with sisters during retreats I have given to their congregation over a number of years which were then pondered privately in prayer.

This is intimately connected with Fr. Haggerty's chapter 10, "Suffering and Trial". One of the great points of discussion among Christologists a few years back was the question of suffering in God. Scripture seems to make it quite clear that there are various motives offered by Scripture for human pain: eschatology; pedagogy; punishment; purification; redemption, and the Cross of Jesus Christ. There is no visceral pessimism here or buried grief. Fr. Haggerty is teaching a hard lesson. We might note Saint Ignatius' ideal that only God knows what he would accomplish in souls were he not hindered in the process. A like-sounding high principle of the modern Evangelical theologian J. Moltmann states that original sin is not so much the titanic desire to be like God as, rather, the refusal to be what God likes! Our *fiat* to God does not give God permission to torment us; there is asked of all the baptized a profound surrender and not just resignation.

In summary: "By his wounds, ours are healed" (cf. Is 53:5; 1 Pet 2:24): as with the prophet Hosea, we may be struck down, but the Lord will bandage our wounds! (6:2); the thoughts of the author indicate that the stigmata of life provide God with openings for his blessings:

> A deeper love for God is inseparable from being wounded over time. Only by a divine wound does

our love for God intensify. This is in part a wound of inner discontent within our soul.

[Quoting Augustin Guillerand] Someone wounds our soul with a wound which will never heal, and it is through that wound that He finds His way to the very center of our being.

Jesus' words in Matthew 25 move us only when understood quite literally in their meaning. Then it is realized that his promise has been kept. He invites us to touch his presence personally in the poor, to clasp the wounds of his crucifixion in the bodies of the poor.

Fr. Haggerty's text is a rewarding work for anyone striving to deepen his spiritual life.

> Timothy Cardinal Dolan
> Archbishop of New York
> September 17, 2012

Introduction

"Love does not always heed the desires of those whom it loves."

—Augustín Guillerand

The desire for deeper relations with God is an aspiration for everyone who takes God seriously. The question remains nonetheless how to pursue more intensely a passion for God. Certainly some practice of interior prayer is necessary for a soul's intimacy with God. In the Catholic tradition there are many fine books teaching methods of silent prayer in order to get started. There are fewer works addressing the deeper issues that arise as one perseveres in prayer and the pursuit of God. The best sources for such questions are found in the classical spiritual treatises, for instance in the writings of the great Carmelite saints Saint John of the Cross and Saint Teresa of Avila, or in Saint Francis de Sales, or in a work like the anonymous *Cloud of Unknowing*. Contemporary works that explain the teachings of the spiritual masters can be also very useful, such as those of the late Fr. Thomas Dubay.

This book tries a different approach and method. Rather than a systematic presentation, the book opts for brief, concentrated observations on aspects of a life with God. The choice to write in concise fragments offers a possible light. Prayer and the interior life are often aided by intuitive graces of deeper awareness. These moments of spiritual insight are usually glimpses at truth in a partial manner, permitting only a brief appraisal, resisting longer analysis. The style of presentation tries to follow this pattern of real experience. The brevity of comment may prove provocative, allowing the reader to refine a thought with a further reflection. The choice to call these "contemplative provocations" is deliberate. It has been common in the Church's tradition to distinguish religious congregations as contemplative or active. The former are enclosed behind monastic walls and give themselves more exclusively to prayer, while active congregations engage in various works in the world. But what does it mean to speak of a *soul* becoming contemplative? This question is not answered simply by reference to the external setting of a life. An environment of solitude and silence may enhance the life of prayer. But it does not determine whether by God's grace a soul becomes contemplative. Contemplative life is not bound, as it were, by geographical restrictions or the external conditions of a life.

What, then, is necessary for a contemplative life? What are the requisite spiritual demands that place a soul on this path? Are there interior obstacles and thresholds in any spiritual progression into contemplative life? Are there false versions of this quest? Are there significant points of spiritual awareness that aid a soul to respond better to the graced invitation to a contemplative life? What is the spiritual secret behind the graces we call contemplative?

If we seek the essential truth of a contemplative life, it is an interior quality of soul that makes a life contemplative. In its simplest meaning, this word contemplative is a descriptive term for a life given fully to God. It involves of course a committed exercise of daily interior prayer. But a soul becomes contemplative most of all by giving to God a complete gift of itself. This inevitably entails a response to quite exacting demands of divine love and, equally, a growing experience of poverty in self. Much of this book seeks to uncover and disclose aspects of these demands.

There is another startling truth that is constant in contemplative lives. It is present as a unifying theme within the book. This is the provocation of God's concealment to the soul. The contemplative life draws its passion and drive in large part from the pursuit of a loving God who hides and is always beyond grasp. This hiddenness of God, even in his immediacy and near presence to the soul, provokes the searching quest of a contemplative soul for God. The concealment of God is, as well, a source of trial and suffering in contemplative lives. In a striking description Saint John of the Cross captures this truth of divine concealment as a provocation to the spiritual life.

> You do very well, O soul, to seek him ever as one hidden, for you exalt God immensely and approach very near him when you consider him higher and deeper than anything you can reach. . . . I mean that you should never desire satisfaction in what you understand about God, but in what you do not understand about him. Never stop with loving and delighting in your understanding and experience of God, but love and delight in what is neither understandable nor perceptible of him. Such is the way, as we said, of seeking him in faith. However surely it may seem you find, experience, and understand God, you must, because he is inaccessible and concealed, always regard him as hidden, and serve him who is hidden in a secret way. (*The Spiritual Canticle* 1.12)

We enter already with these words the deeper waters of spirituality. Although it is advisable in any subject to begin with fundamentals and the basics, we are choosing here to skip the preliminaries, so to speak, and plunge into serious matters from the start. The assumption is that some souls hunger precisely for a true contemplative intimacy with

God and want to be pushed in this direction. These are souls who have already learned much of prayer and virtuous living and need now to extend their response to God.

The premise in all these reflections is that God is inviting us to a deeper interior life. It is possible that many souls miss the beauty of this divine summons to deepen their love. Sometimes we are simply too active and do not value sufficiently the importance of time for prayer. A perennial need within the Church is that more souls become contemplative, not just those in monasteries or cloisters, but hidden souls of prayer living in the world, mixing with the world, a leaven sanctifying it. This need to seek God with passion marks every period of the Church's history, even as it draws little notice. It intensifies with the passage of time.

The first chapter is an entry into the provocation of God's hidden presence to the soul. Many of these initial reflections are a preparation for what follows. The next two chapters on faith's passion and its experience of darkness may be the most challenging. They seek to ground the truth of God's concealed intimacy to the soul in the experiential nature of faith. Faith's experience of a combination of blindness and certitude is steadily reaffirmed in the Catholic tradition from Saint Gregory of Nyssa and pseudo-Dionysius in the patristic period through Saint Thomas Aquinas and Saint

John of the Cross in later centuries. And it is always present in the contemplative experience—corresponding to God's concealment to the soul. The subsequent chapters on contemplative purifications, on the dilemmas of mind and emotion in prayer, and on aberrations in prayer, all engage to some degree the spiritual experience of God's concealment as a condition for greater intimacy with him. By the latter portion of the book the questions of interior poverty and sacrifice and suffering, and finally, of God's hidden presence in the poor, are addressed once again under the rubric of God's concealment to the soul that loves him.

Finally, it ought to be said that these reflections have not only the stimulus behind them of Carmelite works and lesser known works such as those of the Carthusian Augustín Guillerand. The spiritual influence of real persons is also present. A larger number of these thoughts have some link to my contact with Mother Teresa's Missionaries of Charity. Many observations on these pages had a beginning in conversations with sisters during retreats I have given to their congregation over a number of years which were then pondered privately in prayer. In these "provocations" I have often refined in expression what I received from souls much closer to God than they seem to realize.

Mother Teresa wanted her sisters to be "contemplatives in the heart of the world". Everyone who learns to love prayer will hear in this phrase a personal invitation. We need not leave the world, so to speak, to aspire to a deep life of prayer. My gratitude in these pages is to God and the many lives I have known who have given witness to the importance of prayer. In the ways of spirituality we are always indebted to other souls. Our spiritual life is in the end an accumulation of gifts extended to us from the hand of God.

I

The Concealment of God

"To find God is to seek him unceasingly. Here, indeed, to seek is not one thing and to find another. The reward of the search is to go on searching. The soul's desire is fulfilled by the very fact of its remaining unsatisfied, for really to see God is never to have had one's fill of desiring him."

— Saint Gregory of Nyssa

"The hidden God, the mysterious God, is not distant and absent: He is always the God who is near."

— Henri de Lubac, S.J.

"When one comes closer to grasp it the hand draws back."

— Saint Thérèse of Lisieux

Jesus surely had a favorite game as a child, the game of hide and seek. Every child is familiar with this game; every adult remembers it. Even as a grown man, however, Jesus never ceased to play this game in a most serious manner. He continues to do so as the incarnate Son who hides and must be sought. We must seek him always in his hiding. In one sense all of spiritual life, all the deeper riches and poverty of a contemplative life, depends on persevering in this holy game.

". . . Then he also went, not publicly, but as it were in secret" (Jn 7:10). This preference for hiddenness, for remaining unseen, seems to have been a definite impulse of Jesus, clearly depicted on a few occasions in the gospel. It appears he wanted to go unobserved during certain interludes, to pass shrouded through the crowds, inconspicuous and ordinary, even after he began his public life. Surely this desire to remain unrecognized cannot have been a capricious gesture. What is happening here, since in other places he is intent on revealing himself? Does it give hint of a divine attribute which we have not named properly, and yet of vital importance for knowing God's relations with our soul? These occasions when he desired to be remain concealed and unnoticed, are they showing us the shape and contour, as it were, of the only encounter with God at times available to us? Must we necessarily seek him in his hiddenness if we are to find him?

~

"Where have you hidden, Beloved,

and left me moaning?
You fled like the stag
After wounding me;
I went out calling you, and you were gone."

—Saint John of the Cross,
The Spiritual Canticle 1.1

A soul would not ask this question except that
God had shown himself before disappearing. The
departure provoked anguish because an intimacy
preceded it. If God withdraws and conceals himself, we ought not to question why he hides, or,
worse, interpret his hiding as a sign of losing his
love. We should beg only that he reveal his hiding
place so that we may go there in search of him. The
lover who speaks in the poem of Saint John of the
Cross has no thought of losing her beloved's love,
only of finding him again. It is his return that con-
sumes her, not any doubt of his love. And this place
of hiding, she wonders—is it faraway or nearby?

~

Even in the consolation that silent prayer may
grant, there is always a deeper layer of spiritual
need untouched by peace, unsoothed by the tran-
quil breeze. This recess of poverty in the soul longs
for a companion still not seen. It craves for more

than the passing satisfaction. Our gratitude ought to increase if we leave prayer aware of this unsatisfied desire for the one who continues to conceal himself. Perhaps it is the finer grace of prayer.

~

The law of divine concealment is inescapable in all deeper prayer. No contact with God in prayer, no spiritual experience or encounter, does not quickly hide him again. He manages always to flee. Every spiritual taste and discovery becomes dissatisfying before very long. Every comfort received in prayer is impermanent, every light is temporary. But what is remarkable is that our soul's desire can remain firm and unyielding, waiting for God to show himself, the shadows finally lifted. This may be the most unnoticed grace in prayer: we are drawn back constantly despite every difficulty and frustration.

~

Only partial understandings of God's love are ever given, and these are never stable. This can provoke spiritual confusion. The experience of God's hiding can entangle our soul in a morass of useless questioning. Indeed, if we commit ourselves to praying in a solitary silence for a sufficient period of our life, we may think sometimes that God's hiding is the most familiar mark of his divine personality. But we ought to learn over time that a concealed presence is his manner of keeping companionship. His disguises are his way of manifesting fidelity and love.

～

God is more present in prayer than we may often think, turning toward us with a father's solicitude to protect our soul in some manner, assuaging some doubt, removing some uncertainty. In this there may be no image, no emotion, no particular thought. Yet the effect within our soul is a certitude that God is very personal in his love. He asks us to trust this truth.

～

The simple truth is that God is perplexing in his love. It is the paradox of more intimate relations with him. Unfortunately we may stop too soon on the path that leads more deeply into his love. Our experience in prayer can cause us to halt prematurely. God's preference for hiding does not match our expectation of intimacy with him. His presence to us in prayer offers no easy assurances of his love. Indeed God may seem painfully unknown when he is sought most intensely. It can be as though we induce him to hide when we desire him most. We know him sometimes only as he leaves behind sharp hungers in our soul.

~

A tension between God's disclosure of himself and his hiddenness is always present in our relations with God. For reasons we never fully fathom, God determines the pace and the extent to which he uncovers any glimpse of his face. This is unique and personal for each soul; yet certain patterns are recurring. These point to the partial nature of every experience of divine love and the return by God afterward to deeper mystery. A rhythm of divine approach and disappearance repeats continually. This interchange educates us in the paradox of relations with God. When God is drawing closer, it is not uncommon that darkness encloses the soul for a time. Trials become precursors to deeper graces in prayer. More significantly, the purifications God imposes parallel the disclosure God is preparing. When he shows himself, it will be in camouflage and shadow, the glimpse of his face often not recognized until later. The pattern extends outside prayer, too. A poor man's face, uncomprehended at the time, leaves our soul disquieted, longing for God and not knowing why. After every instance of showing himself, Our Lord disappears again from sight, a further provocation to spiritual hunger.

～

We may know that God will not allow himself to be apprehended easily, but sometimes we forget the complementary truth. Once he is known to some degree, he will not permit us to keep at a distance on limited terms, maintaining a prudential respect. He is a hidden God, but when he deigns to show himself, he demands afterward our passionate pursuit.

～

Perhaps the saints became holy because they never made peace with the impossibility of seeing God in this life. Among the poor, or in the midst of hostile or indifferent souls, they went in search of his face, only to return again to the silence of prayer where God once more hid himself. These souls lived as though always on the verge of finding a treasure and never succeeding. Blind and groping, cast back into darkness after refusing every partial vision— this was always preferable to taking comfort in a brilliant shadow.

～

We learn the hidden mystery of God in the presence of the Eucharist, or perhaps not at all. Kneeling in silence before the quiet of a tabernacle we can come to know a deeper longing for God, sometimes a strange and poor longing. God speaks untranslatable words in that silence. A tone and manner is recognized more often than any message. Those silent hours may cast our soul into an ocean of incomprehension; or they may be like tripping over sharp stones through a shallow rivulet. But without such hours, our faith stands at the shoreline, perhaps admiring the view, but rarely touching water.

∼

Can we persevere in love for someone we do not see? This is an essential religious question; in part, it determines whether we will continue to pray in a manner that leads to the interior poverty of contemplative graces.

∼

Some days in prayer God may seem as though never to leave, and then, without warning, the shadows sweep in like a thick fog over a coastland, brushing against one's soul, confusing it. And yet the desire to continue praying can remain, strong and resolute. This determination not to depart from prayer surely confirms that God has not at all left our company. He simply hides in the cover and haze that now obscures him from view.

~

God is never so hidden for long, provided our eyes are open. Indeed no one grows in faith without finding signs of God's help and intervention in daily life, small favors that could be dismissed as chance until we begin to notice their frequency. Fragmentary, perhaps, seemingly unlinked, these quiet signs reveal a personality of great kindness in God. But even more, they may reinforce the pain of those times when his concealment seems to be again steady and enduring.

~

Christian revelation is the mystery of divine personhood gazing at us from a human face. Yet it may be that sometimes in prayer we embrace an idea of God's mystery in too exaggerated a manner and forget to keep our eyes on Jesus of Nazareth—even if no exchange of glances takes place and we are finally left staring at someone departing. The mystery of the eternal God hides in that human face. Often it must be sought where the divinity of Jesus Christ was most concealed, in the hours at Calvary when his face was marred and disfigured and he spoke for long interludes nothing but from his eyes.

~

We can assume in faith that some form of divine self-disclosure is taking place whenever a genuine encounter with God occurs in prayer. But this is often not anything we have enjoyed, in thought or feeling. Sometimes, when God wants us to know him better, he may disclose himself as a mystery even more incomprehensible than our previous ignorance seemed to indicate.

~

To say that the face of God is perpetually concealed expresses a truth. But the metaphor might be completed by insisting that the sound of his breathing can still be heard in the darkness that sometimes hides him.

~

Will Saint Veronica have restored one day the veil that mesmerized her eyes? One would think not, precisely because it could never satisfy. And yet it is not simply an image that will fail to satiate fully. The excess of divine love emanating from the face of Jesus will always extend beyond us, even in heaven. The face of the man of Nazareth will remain in a certain sense eternally impenetrable, pointing toward what our human eyes can never fully perceive.

∼

The inclination to hiddenness is a quiet mark of holiness. It corresponds to the secrecy of relations between a soul and God. For it seems to be God's consistent habit with souls to conceal himself even when they are close to him. We can surmise that the saints came to know well this divine preference for concealment. It added intensity to their seeking after God in his many disguises. Rather than frustrating them, the divine hiding provoked them with intense longings. And it aroused in them a desire for their own concealment, not from God, but from the eyes of others, so that they might remain among the unknown and the unrecognized. If we want to find holiness, the first place to search is in the shadows and corners.

∼

If we desire deeper prayer, should we not also learn to pass through the crowds in secret, unnoticed by others, drawing no attention? The desire to be unknown and hidden, concealed from sight, is not simply a monkish inclination. It is an impulse that arises with deeper prayer. This desire has a certain logic in the nature of love. We seek in love a God who has a penchant for hiding himself, and we are drawn to follow him into his own hiding places.

~

The chance to savor God's hidden presence in the Eucharist for the quiet privilege alone—leaving behind the noise of streets at an unplanned hour, entering the subdued hush behind a closing church door, kneeling in the shadows before a lit red lamp and the tabernacle—the sudden desire to be near God in an empty church may be an anticipation of deeper longings in prayer.

2

Faith's Passion

"You are a mystery as deep as the sea; the more I search, the more I find, and the more I find, the more I search for you. But I can never be satisfied; what I receive will ever leave me desiring more. When you fill my soul I have an even greater hunger, and I grow more famished for your light. I desire above all to see you, the true light, as you really are."

—Saint Catherine of Siena

"The knowledge of faith does not set desire at rest, but inflames it—because everyone desires to see what he believes."

—Saint Thomas Aquinas

"Never speak of God from memory, never speak of him as of someone absent."

—Maurice Blondel

We ought not to confuse a deeper conviction in faith with a complacency in religious belief. The assurance of correct belief does not deepen relations with God in prayer. Correct belief is not in itself an impetus to prayer. God must be sought with passion, in a profound spirit of searching. Otherwise his hiddenness in mystery invites reducing his personal mystery to abstract notions. All thought of God that remains simply an intellectual exercise, even to gain proper knowledge, misses an essential element in faith. Faith is never exclusively an attitude of mind. It engages our whole being. It must be driven by spiritual passion.

The mystery of a personal God is the source of prayer. But because his divine mystery is beyond our conception, we are likely to experience a certain strain in our reflections on his nature and truth. God seems at times to parry off our attempts to understand him, resisting our effort to take hold of him in a moment's fragile thought. Behind this may be God's refusal to be reduced to an item of mere thought and observation. He desires to be personally sought in love. Without love animating our seeking, no effort of thought alone gets nearer to him. What may be surprising, however, is that our passion for God can increase as we encounter his greater mystery. This spiritual passion may flame up after pondering a truth of God has, for a time, frustrated our mind. After the struggle of thought, we must accept a silencing of thought before the concealed face of God. It is a sign, perhaps, that our passion for God is intensifying in prayer.

~

It is not long before we realize that great satisfactions do not await our intellect as we pursue the knowledge of God. The contrary is the evident rule. Every truth about God, embraced after labored reflection or in a swift insight, is soon perceived to extend beyond what we have grasped in thought. A backlash of incomprehension follows every deeper insight we receive about God in prayer. The incomprehension is often the greater grace, more than the knowledge we may have gained of God. It protects us from resting in an intellectual comfort as the fruit of prayer, and thereby halting our search for God. Other times an intuition is given. The search to know God, the perpetual incompletion of this quest, teaches a deeper truth about the God of love who has become a man. We discover for ourselves how quickly an infinite light overwhelms every lesser light. Every glimpse of his truth draws us into a more piercing awareness of how little we still know. We realize he is known even in his human Incarnation as the beloved one who stretches always beyond our understanding.

~

Some minds cannot countenance an ignorance before the mystery of God as a healthy condition of soul. What cannot be embraced as true about God except in a humble act of submission grates on them. The perplexity that accompanies a mystery of faith seems an obstacle to faith. Some souls would quickly remove it if they could. They do not realize that a blind, unseeing quality is a necessity for more intense faith. It must permeate the certitudes of our faith in God.

∼

A rational tendency in faith can provide a persuasive clarity that pleases the mind, but sometimes at a greater loss. Too much rationality, too much assurance of taking hold of divine truths, may deflect our awareness from the deeper personal mystery of Our Lord still unknown, still calling in a quiet manner for our desire and humble seeking—and for prayer before a tabernacle.

∼

The desire to possess our religious belief in a kind of unassailable security ought to be restrained if we seek a deeper conviction in faith. More intense faith begins after our knowledge of God is no longer so clear and satisfying as it may have been previously. Our soul has arrived at a threshold. All desire to see openly, without obstruction, must be relinquished. Only then do we embrace the mystery of God with a firmer certitude of faith. Our contact with God in faith may be more blind. But our faith also possesses a greater sureness in the truth it embraces, a truth, as always, united to the Church's assent in faith. This submission cannot occur without intellectual mortifications, without refusals to lean greedily toward answers that may comfort our mind for a time, but leave God himself as a real presence disengaged from all we are thinking. Without a deeper surrender of our intellect in this manner, there will be restless, fitful searching on our part, a chasing after God unpeacefully instead of a more complete gift of ourselves to him.

∼

God is very patient, it seems, toward our presumption of knowing him when we keep superficial relations with him. He surely requires, however, a more humble realization of how ignorant we have been before he stretches toward us the deeper truth of his incomprehensibility to our soul. Every approach of our soul closer to the mystery of God entails a humbling of intelligence, not more impressive thoughts.

∼

The transcendence of the divine nature, completely other than our human nature, is a truth requiring a periodic recovery within our prayer. But unless it provokes as well a need to discover someone presently at home within our soul, this truth can be transposed into an erroneous idea of an extreme unknowability in God. An excessive notion of God's infinite mystery can seem equivalent to the impossibility of personal relations with him. This is only our own thought getting in the way of God's actual, concealed presence in the silence of our prayer.

∼

God's incomprehensible mystery, in other words, eludes us if considered exclusively as a source of intellectual frustration. It is never an abstract notion. On the contrary, his incomprehensibility is part of our encounter with God. It may seem at first inexplicable that we can deepen our love for God precisely when we intuitively sense how much we do not know him. But even then, not knowing him in a certain sense, we can surrender to him. His personal presence we may not feel at all. We may not be able to hold a clear thought of him in our mind. Nonetheless God is known inasmuch as we give ourselves to him. A surrender in love unites our soul to God. And in a mysterious manner we can know this in prayer. The effect on the soul of such an act is immensely different from that of staring alone in darkness at what may seem the absence or disappearance of God.

~

Faith today faces a challenge in the modern culture of technology, which in turn is also an obstacle to contemplative life. The problem is not technology in itself, but a certain poverty of spiritual intelligence resulting from a predominant exercise of mind. The drive for efficiency and practical advantage can become a primary quest of intelligence. But this habit of mind closes the human soul to the more elusive and invisible realm of God and his revelation. While God is the ultimate truth to be sought, it is difficult to experience a need for him while keeping steady companionship with a computer. By means of the machine, one is supposed to become wise. But what kind of wisdom is this? Taking hold of truth is easily identified with discoveries of pragmatic usefulness or the acquisition of fact and information. This narrow search for practical benefit suffocates a deeper hunger of the human soul. The struggle for religious insight and for God, unanswerable at the touch of a keyboard, can be neglected provided the electricity continues to flow. In this sense the new century is a new era. The challenge to faith may not be primarily from an aggressive rejection of God. In a culture of technology the question of God can be simply ignored as lacking practical purpose, a wasteful glance at fanciful vapors.

~

It is not only ignoring God that keeps him from us. To think about God in a detached manner, treating him as an object of scrutiny and examination, is to invite a false perception about God. An impersonal abstraction replaces the living God. A more honest thought of God requires engagement with his divine presence. This is fully possible only in prayer. Our most valuable reflections about God occur during prayer, as they simplify and become more intuitive, less analytical. A gaze from eternity seems at times to touch these thoughts. It has the effect of leaving our thought subdued and overcome, sometimes overwhelmed. This is a sign of approaching closer to a more truthful thought of God.

~

There are questions about God which can persist in our mind for their enigmatic quality, like puzzles which remain still undeciphered. God's timeless knowledge or the predestination of the soul might be examples. They should perhaps be left aside after a time, not because we give up finding answers, but because our thought after a while has no love when we return to them. Other sacred mysteries of faith can be very different. They too overwhelm our intelligence, but not simply as enigmas that resist explanation. The mysteries of Jesus Christ as God and man, and his real presence in the Eucharist, are beyond a perfectly clear explanation. Yet they can attract us in a profound manner. It is a different kind of frustration they provoke. It is never simply intellectual, but one which stirs love. The difficulty they cause is the difficulty of unattained love.

～

When a person concludes any period of theological study with a sharper awareness of the mysteries in Catholic faith, mysteries not reducible to explanations in words, it is surely because the soul prayed during this time. A real encounter with God in prayer accompanied the effort of intellectual work.

～

A correct conceptual idea about God is not the same as a true thought about God. The former may be an accurate doctrinal affirmation or an insightful theological clarification. A true thought of God, however, includes an awareness of his presence in the current hour. It is easy to take up an idea about God while oblivious to the reality of his actual presence in the present moment. But a recognition of his presence is always more decisive for relations with him. How easy, however, to reverse the importance and seek a satisfaction regarding God that feeds only the intellect's need.

~

Some of the finer spiritual intuitions can be received only in a humble incomprehension. Only an act of surrender to God uncovers these truths. His personal kindness and solicitude toward one's soul, for instance, is never the discovery simply of a probing reflection. The deeper realization takes place more likely as a sudden, unexpected surprise, usually after a period of searching for God. Afterward, this certitude of God's love retains an indecipherable element, still unexplained and unknown in some manner. It can never be subject to analysis. It is not recovered simply by returning to a thought. Only further submissions to God bring once again the awareness of his very personal care.

3

Faith's Blindness

"Do we therefore suppose that we have understood? It is not argument which makes us understand these things, but sanctity; if indeed what is
incomprehensible can be in any way understood."

—Saint Bernard

"Those who understand God more, understand
more distinctly the infinitude which remains to be
understood; whereas those who see less of Him
do not realize so clearly what remains to be seen."

—Saint John of the Cross

"Have we said anything, uttered any sound, which
is worthy of God?"
—Saint Augustine

*A certain ignorance of God accompanies our knowledge
of God in faith. This statement appears initially to be a
self-contradiction. But it merely acknowledges that what
we know of God from Christian revelation does not arrive
at the fullness of his divine truth. The true nature of God*

remains always beyond our grasp. The contemplative life involves a daily engagement with this constraint upon our knowledge of God. The closer proximity to God given in prayer accentuates the experience of God's transcendent mystery. It is the person of prayer who knows God more intensely as one who is unknown. The paradox is central to all contemplative life.

There is an irony about faith stressed by Saint John of the Cross. It reflects the truth of God's concealment even as he is sought with greater fervor. While more intense faith deepens certitude in the soul, it also brings darkness to the mind. The latter does not mean that doubts arise, nor that irresolvable questions intrude into prayer. Questions would imply a curiosity, a seeking of one's intelligence after God. Rather, as faith advances, the certitude of faith increases. But precisely then a strange dullness of mind may permeate our thought of God in prayer. This peculiar blunting of thought about God can become familiar in prayer. At first it makes no sense; nor can it be overcome. An insight is necessary, and the recognition of a pattern. An impotence of thought before the mystery of God often precedes an act of deeper love for God in prayer. Difficulty in thinking about God, rather than simply a frustration, becomes a provocation to love. Our mind's incapacity for the plenitude of God becomes a condition for the advancement of our soul's love for God. In the dark certitudes of faith, in shadows that are alive with his presence, love seeks God blindly, with more intense longing.

∼

Greater certitude in faith while undergoing an impotence of thought might seem incompatible. Or it might sound as though one is embracing convictions that have no reasonable basis. In fact, however, this link is consistent with the nature of faith's assent to Christian revelation. Revealed truths of the Catholic faith are presented in the clear, precise language of doctrinal propositions. As statements employing concepts they can be understood, and we assent in faith to them. Nonetheless the truths these propositions affirm constitute inexhaustible mysteries. They concern the reality of God in ways that ultimately stretch beyond our comprehension. The propositions of faith are intelligible as true statements and essential to the act of believing. At the same time, however, the expression in human language of the revealed truth is inept for grasping who God really is. This is a cause of tension in our experience of faith. The clarity of a doctrinal proposition can deflect our mind from fully realizing the ultimate transcendence of the mystery it is affirming. The actual mystery may diminish in wonder to the degree it is encountered in words that offer a semblance of comprehension. A corrective is called for. Understanding what we believe, even in limited manner, is of course necessary. But another aspect of believing is equally important. When faith deepens, it is precisely the mystery in God that must animate the soul's search. Encounter with the personal mystery of God must become the soul's dominant need.

∼

Is a true and accurate thought about God an obstacle to realizing more fully the hidden mystery of God? Would a leap into a cloud of darkness surrounding God assure a more direct experience of the living God? Clearly not on both counts. The propositions of faith in their clarity are indispensable for assenting to the content of divine revelation. But not simply for a proper belief. Something else occurs in the act of faith besides an exposure to conceptual truths about God. As we grow in faith, we are granted a deeper certitude toward God when assenting to the propositions of faith. It is the certitude of coming into contact with the living presence of God. This experience of certitude is indeed a reflection of God giving himself to our soul. It is an experiential confirmation of the truth of our faith.

∼

If we recall in prayer that God is infinite in his being, timeless, immutable—and exquisitely personal—these truths of the divine nature are bound at times to freeze our intelligence. The mystery of the divine nature flees beyond our mind. But it is only a portion of our mind that is overwhelmed. Another awareness, of adoration and prostration, is possible. An unfathomed goodness is present in a God who is infinite in his love. We need not ponder this truth with perplexity even as the notion of infinity in God will always vanquish our intelligence. It is true that any reflection we make can be only a paltry attempt incapable of grasping the divine mystery. The concealment of his nature always remains. On the other hand, something else takes place besides our realization that God is beyond our grasp. Our longing to know him is in itself a real entry into light. Our certitude of his goodness and love is not a forced assurance on our part. Not only is it profoundly correct, but God confirms this truth precisely by intensifying our longing for him.

$\sim$

The incomprehensibility of God should not be reduced to a psychological experience. If ever we focus too intently on the unknowability of God, we may plunge our soul inwardly upon itself, toward caverns within the psyche where only a gloomy absence of meaning is met. This would be a kind of visceral reaction to a false idea about God. It is true to speak of the mind's inability to comprehend God. But this incapacity does not imply that God is aloof and absent. On the contrary, his love and goodness, infinite as they are, invite our confident turn in love toward him. At the same time his love is so far beyond the capacity of thought that we have but one recourse. We must aspire to surrender to him our whole being. He must be approached by our giving ourselves in a manner also beyond our current comprehension.

∼

The experience of faith's obscurity that accompanies prayer may seem to some to resemble the darkness of unbelief. But these experiences are vastly different. Deeper faith provokes a more intense desire for God precisely in a soul that has become more blind and unknowing. The intellect in this case remains aflame with desire. On the other hand, the darkness that comes from unbelief produces a fatigue and weariness of mind, and sometimes a bitterness toward the notion of religious truth, an altogether different frustration of intelligence.

∼

If it is correct, then, to declare that the divine nature is hidden and ultimately inaccessible to our mind's limited capacity, this truth needs to be balanced always by remembrance that God is utterly personal toward our soul. The mystery of God is of love and goodness, not of inscrutability. Infinite mystery in God does not mean that he is unapproachable in his divinity. He has shown us quite the opposite in his Incarnation as the man of Nazareth. Indeed, Jesus himself is always accessible to our soul. We need only turn in a state of need to him.

～

Clearly, then, the idea we have of God can make prayer difficult, if not impossible. We block our way to God by every wrong notion of God. That can happen if we dwell too much on God's transcendent mystery, if we look upon him as distant and remote, as a God without eyes. A God unavailable to our pleading is a distortion of God. Yet this can be a temptation sometimes, to conceive his hiddenness as an absence. Neglecting his personal presence, we may tend ourselves to become impersonal with God. Approaching him too much as unknown, we may think we have become unknown to him, that he has forgotten us. The private thought of God's absence is simply mistaken and must be countered. Otherwise prayer will suffer, even collapse. The mystery of God may be beyond understanding. But it is certain that he listens to us in silence. It is the only way we can pray, trusting that he waits on every sincere word released from our heart.

~

All the same the discomfort of not really knowing God cannot be evaded, unless we prefer to give up praying. But if we accustom ourselves to this darkened state of mind in prayer, and accept it, the submission has a way of drawing our soul to God. It is not an ordinary knowledge that is bestowed then with grace. Rather, a kind of unclaimable, indefinite recognition occurs. A sure awareness of God's deeper presence to the soul accompanies any darkness of our mind. With that awareness it becomes clear that the hidden presence of God is not at all an absence. It is quite the contrary of an absence. God concealed and hidden is God present to our soul in hiding. God has not forsaken us when shadows seem to becloud and blind us. The lack of sight may be a condition of prayer. But it does not reflect the deeper truth of God's engagement with the soul. In darkness and obscurity we encounter a deeper mystery of the divine presence, embraced in a greater intensity of faith.

〜

This way of knowing God in darkness has been called a knowledge by unknowing, as confusing as that phrase initially sounds. It reflects the paradox of deeper relations with God in prayer. A sense of separation and distance from God may for a while intensify in prayer rather than an experience of closer contact with him. The divine mystery can become more dense and unfathomable as mystery. Deeper relations with God may accentuate how unknowable God is. We may seem to know less of God than previously. Yet this is not a backward regression into real ignorance, nor an absence of knowledge. The soul advances by more intense faith and love deeper into truth. It realizes with acute sharpness that the nature of God exceeds comprehension, that he is beyond reflection. To touch the edge of that awareness is not to arrive at a conclusion after a sequence of thoughts. God as someone still unknown seizes the soul in prayer, without an understanding of how this takes place. The truth of God as still unknown cuts like the blade of a knife the sinews of the mind.

〜

There is something else in this knowledge of God. It takes hold of consciousness unlike other forms of knowledge. This knowledge of God does not pass thresholds to particular moments of clarity and apprehension. It is not a knowledge that builds by accumulation. It cannot be examined for its weight and significance. It has rather a qualitative effect, in a subtle manner. Knowledge of God permeates attention and influences perception. God's living presence becomes a background to daily vision. God is watching and protecting and inviting. The different mode of awareness is a form of knowing, a kind of perpetual anticipation felt toward someone unseen and expected.

∼

Only when we are more united in love to God, then, does he favor us with a more intense awareness of his concealment. The deeper realization of his unknowability is a gift accompanying every advancement in love. God offers the one with the other. Like a secret exchanged between lovers, God makes his transcendent otherness the secret known without our being able to claim this as a knowledge in the usual sense. So we come away from such prayer with nothing particular in thought other than wanting God and desiring to give ourselves to him. The prayer may not seem so graced from the side of the soul, certainly not in knowing God, who is sealed in mystery more than ever. Yet the certitude of faith has intensified in this blindness. The effect is to increase a longing for God that lingers after prayer as a need to search for him.

4

Contemplative Beginnings

"In order to draw nearer the divine ray the intellect must advance by unknowing rather by the desire to know, and by blinding itself and remaining in darkness rather than by opening its eyes."

—Saint John of the Cross

"To be aware that you are accompanied, but not to know the One who accompanies you, is a dreadful mystery."

—Marguerite Castillon

"You can know something which you are unaware you know."

—Saint Augustine

A trial of interior purification in prayer introduces a soul to the contemplative life. The experience is consistent with the paradox of a God who has revealed himself and yet remains incomprehensible in his divine truth. In drawing closer to our soul God will show himself now in a more painful manner as one who is still unknown and hidden.

The irony is a provocation for a soul of prayer. A pruning takes place at the hand of God which induces a soul to seek him more intensely. Purification at the outset of contemplative prayer is explicable only in this light. We experience in a more direct manner, by way of trial, the hiddenness of a God who has made his home within our own human soul.

Contemplative life is initiated undramatically—one might say in a concealed, subtle, confusing manner. One symptom is a dry discomfort in prayer like the bodily ache of a fever that does not subside. The aridity contrasts with the prior experience of prayer, when a consoling sense of God's presence was enjoyed. Now there is little felt contact with God, nothing savored in emotion. God seems to disappear more and more into hiding. Other symptoms as well seem incongruous as signs of a growth in prayer. A focused attention on Our Lord becomes difficult. Noisy distractions disturb prayer. Petty concerns interfere with prayer and replace quiet reflections about God. The gospel pages no longer offer vivid attraction. Anxious thoughts and unwelcome memories intrude, and the mind is unable to settle down. The struggle for an attentive silence and some serenity can burden an entire period of prayer. The sense of being alone, somehow separated from God, unable to pray, does not let up.

~

It may seem that something has gone spiritually wrong, that unfaithfulness and neglect have damaged relations with God. The general malaise, it is thought, must be due to offending God in some way. Wrongs committed, minor failures and mistakes, become exceedingly troubling. The insecurity spreads beyond prayer, causing at times scrupulosity. Firmer resolutions in virtue are made, but the confusion continues unrelieved. Vigilance in avoiding sin, more sacrifice and self-giving to others, penitential practices—nothing removes the insipid taste in prayer. The spiritual life becomes forced labor, an exercise of willpower out of proportion to ordinary tasks. Perseverance may keep a soul soldiering on. But it is likely to question its suitability for a serious pursuit of God.

~

The return each day to silent prayer in this condition means to face the discomfort of silence. There can be a strong temptation to give up prayer or to find some activity in silent prayer to counter frustration. A more superficial prayer can be adopted which discards the effort of listening in silence to God. One might opt, for instance, to spend time in prayer simply reading. In that case the dryness

and distraction may lift to a degree because they
are less noticed. This may seem to restore relations
with God. It would be a poor exchange, however,
a step backward. The soul would forfeit a grace it
was beginning to taste of a deeper thirst for God.
The thirst of the soul for God is stronger in the
desert. It is easy, nonetheless, to run for the shade.

~

Those who embrace the richer possibilities of silent
prayer walk always a path of paradox. They come to
prayer knowing that Jesus is near and approachable
in a tabernacle, then do not experience him in any
clear manner. They hunger for time alone with
him, then find the desired hour a trial of emptiness and self-doubt. They read Scripture one day
as though hearing words never heard before. The
next day the gospel is cloying and repetitive. In
one hour there is great confidence that God listens
to every thought and desire. The next hour he appears deaf and impervious. For an extended time
he invites a soul closer, and then, as though tired
of its company, hides in a long, silent absence. Perhaps there is no end to these shifts. Certainly they
cannot be anticipated from hour to hour.

~

A stubborn determination not to halt can decide, in a sense, a spiritual destiny. For often this is a prolonged trial of some years. But an insight is also helpful, and perhaps given frequently in grace. The thought may occur to a soul in this condition that a dry desire to love is not at all an absence of love. On the contrary, the dryness is like smoke rising up from a hidden region of fire within the soul. The lack of feeling is only what is consciously experienced. There is a thirst beneath feelings, a thirst enflamed in the heat of the desert, and many souls begin to realize this. The aridity slowly carves a wound, a cauterization at a concealed depth of soul which burns away the inclination to seek one's own satisfactions in love.

~

If in these purifications we find it difficult to approach God in prayer, what may not be noticed is the parallel trial of human relations taking on a drier, more impersonal note. Yet the two are often joined. Outside prayer, too, God brings a taste of impoverishment to our work and into our relations with people, reducing us there as well to a purer intention for himself.

~

In crossing these initial thresholds, there is a desire to remain quiet in prayer. It is not easily accepted, however, as a grace. Silence before a God who is now more hidden seems to risk being alone simply with self. Contemplative prayer can seem at first like a conversation that arrives at a sudden, awkward silence, without words or a thought. We are unaccustomed to this absence of speech and at first dislike it. The emptiness can seem vapid, without purpose. But all these confusions are only symptoms. They await an insight: our own silence is not disagreeable to God, it does not repel him. He listens to the longing deep within our soul. With God we must learn a new language of love in which words are often unnecessary.

~

Tired words leaking from an ashen heart, words that sound like a reproach toward our soul, reminding us what cannot be attained without love —would it not be better to accept defeat and stop praying? Remaining in silence can seem a surrender to emptiness, a refusal of effort. But sometimes no words are necessary to express our desire to God. Our longing for him hides beneath words. A bedraggled, branded spirit may be the reality of the day, the humbling truth of the current hour. But

it does not preclude a cry of love from the silent
core of our being.

~

After a while, if our soul grows in the poverty of
contemplative prayer, silence is simply a veneer of
the divine concealment. It does not keep us from
God's presence; it is not an obstacle in prayer, no
matter how dry or empty it seems. Rather, silence
is itself a kind of veil of love inviting us into a secret
companionship with God. We have only to accept
that this silence is a hiding place for his incursions
of love.

~

There is in a sense no option. One cannot seek
God after a while except inside a greater density
of interior silence in prayer where there is no help
from words, no distinct utterance that would predictably cast open a door. The soul can only wait
in a poverty of speech. This silence, like every real
poverty, is capable of attracting and repelling at the
same time. Sometimes a soul may feel inclined to
rebel against it. To wait upon God without words
can seem to assume his absence to the soul. But the
silence is a true hiding place for God, and he has his
own secret ways of speaking in this silence. Those
who pray in a deeper silence of longing come to

know the attraction of this divine language. They immerse their soul in its secrecy. In the deeper layers of silence, his presence is a mysterious power drawing the soul's poverty and love.

~

All these difficulties can dull a soul's appreciation for the hidden exchange taking place. Even as it is stripped by purification to a painful silence before God, a real contact with God occurs. A naked longing for God burns beneath this silence. The soul may know this only in fitful, uncertain ways. But there is a complementarity of two movements in these contemplative purifications: we are reduced to poverty precisely as God draws nearer. The two things may seem opposed, but only if we forget God's love for poverty in a soul. Impoverishment in prayer means always to fall more deeply under the loving gaze of God.

~

From a detached point of view, it is not difficult to accept that purifications are necessary for a deeper life of prayer. But when souls are passing through the initial trials of contemplative prayer, they may hesitate to trust that the little love they seem in their own view to possess will ever permit God to bring these struggles to a fruitful conclusion.

~

The soul experiencing aridity would be more easily reconciled to this condition if it was not joined at times to an anxiety that God's displeasure for some unknown reason was the cause of it. On the other hand, the purer longing for God beneath feelings is a refinement of the soul's passion and a significant grace in prayer. Aridity exhausts over time an impulse to seek anything in prayer other than God himself. Desires may flare up, but they taper and fade into unimportance as a deeper passion for God more directly engages prayer. Everything less than God becomes simply a poor object for love, and a soul gradually realizes this. In one sense contemplative life from its inception is a routing of every spurious form of love. And it takes place initially through these purifications. The steady burn of aridity brings a new depth of passion and love to prayer. The soul's longing turns more exclusively toward God in prayer when there is nothing other than God to draw desire.

~

Contemplative prayer has its source, then, in an intense passion for God. The strain of wanting God begins to permeate a life, overwhelming other desires. It is in one sense a kind of constraint upon desire, and a discontent within the soul. Prayer becomes a steady, unrelenting passion for someone not possessed, not near enough to be permanently enjoyed, someone who disappears again into hiding after every closer approach. Always a deeper longing in the soul remains unassuaged. Never to appease a quiet, unrelenting need for God, never to find God in a way that would release the soul from searching for him—this is the true measure of contemplative prayer. A notion of prayer that would overcome the concealment of God is deceived. The fire of the soul in prayer burns by not seeing. The flames of the soul's desire for God are stoked in darkness. Without that fire the soul would flee the distant spaces. It would never know the naked passion for God found in the desert among the dry winds and the sands.

~

The beginnings of contemplative life require a faith lived in shadows and darkness, without a clear aspiration other than a deep need to surrender one's soul more fully to God. This faith is lived blindly, in dark certitudes—not because the soul prefers darkness rather than light—but because this darkness is real and unavoidable. It is an intense faith that leans and stretches forward in the silence of prayer to a threshold that is still beyond view. This blind faith allows God to conquer as he chooses, so that the darkness may be perceived in time as luminous with a presence beyond sight. The dark certitudes of faith are the bedrock of contemplative prayer.

~

These purifications can never be anticipated in a way that would exempt a soul and allow an easier accommodation simply because one has been forewarned. Taking God seriously is costly, of course. But this has less to do with confirming spiritual predictions, and more with discovering personally what the loss of self as the gospel describes it actually entails. And yet the truths of deeper prayer are taught to some souls in ways that defy the usual expectation of a need for training. From a human standpoint the knowledge of these purifications would seem to assume an education in spiritual theology or at least some spiritual counsel. But some souls learn God's work in this regard by a humble instinct of the heart, without consultation or the benefit of books. They come to know these purifications and their value almost naturally, like an artist who takes to his art easily even while suffering the pain of seeking beauty. But this, too, is God's hidden work, reflecting his great desire that souls become contemplative.

～

The more serious graces in prayer arrive only after purifications have made forgetting self a steady habit no longer needing arduous effort. But this requires also that outside prayer the sharper edges of self have been sanded down and even crushed. We have to play a part in this, but surely God assumes the primary role. And so the customary pattern of souls undergoing struggles with humiliation and aloneness, facing burdens and demands, and finding no release from trial as they are growing in a deeper life of prayer. What God asks is that we accept the hard truth of actual poverty in itself, the emptiness in everything sought apart from him. It is always a certain desperation of need for God that draws his love in a deeper way.

～

At least in the aftermath, divine purpose is clearly evident in these contemplative purifications. God's ways are anything but arbitrary. The early symptoms of contemplative prayer are so common and regular that they amount to a fixed, predictable pattern. But these symptoms expose, as well, a challenge. They are not just a trial to endure, but an essential recognition waiting to be seen. These purifications are already a sign that in seeking God we can expect to be emptied, diminished, stripped without warning. God will often take from us precisely what we would keep for ourselves. He will deny to us what we most ardently desire. We will lose at times what we assumed to be permanent and stable. These purifications are an early taste of love's demand to relinquish every sense of possession, every desire for anything other than God himself.

5

Emotion in Prayer

"You are not the owner of what you feel. No! You own nothing. You only receive. . . . The hour when we no longer receive is a merciful delicacy of God to allow us our turn to give to Him at last."

—Abbé Henri Huvelin

"When I did not seek him with self-love, he came to me without being sought."

—Saint John of the Cross

"To love, after all, is to give oneself, and to give oneself is to forget oneself."

—Augustín Guillerand

The concealment of God is never confined simply to our mind's engagement with divine truth. The most common experience of God's hiding is an affective one, an experience of his concealment within our emotions and feelings. The heart's deprivation in its desire for God afflicts all

71

who seek a deeper life of prayer. God's purpose in deny-
ing us emotional gratification is in part to purify a self-
seeking impulse in our prayer. In that sense it is a prelim-
inary emptying of our soul prior to greater spiritual gifts.
But it is more than a purification. This experience, too,
confirms the penchant of God to hide himself—even, sur-
prisingly, from our enjoyment of his company.

The desire for an experience of God's presence
may bring us to prayer, but the same impulse, if
not purified, will exact a later cost. If we become
anxious for emotional consolation in prayer, a focus on self can begin to affect the life of solitary
prayer. It becomes incidental to this whether an
hour of prayer is consoling or dissatisfying. The
habitual desire for a gratifying experience will turn
prayer into a self-centered enterprise. Then, in one
of the ironies of spiritual life, a soul that perseveres
in prayer comes away from it more turned toward
self than toward God. This desire for satisfaction in
prayer leads many people simply to give up silent
prayer. Indeed the abandonment of prayer in this
manner by those who aspired to a serious prayer life
is one of the more hidden tragedies in the Church.

～

Emotion incites the imagination. Religious emotion is no different. If we seem to feel God's pres-

ence, the thought may arise that God must be near in that moment. But surely this perception under the sway of emotion appeals also to self-love. Is God actually closer then to the soul? Is he closer than in times of aridity? Perhaps not, although it can be hard to resist the thought. The error can be consequential if it means that we forsake a purer pursuit of God in his transcendent mystery in exchange for sporadic encounters with our own inflamed desire. A sobering corrective is to remember that God in his immensity cannot be contained, held down, possessed within the human heart.

~

To the extent that faith becomes a kind of emotional conviction, an insecurity accompanies our engagement with divine mystery. Relying on an affective experience of faith will demand eruptions of emotional release to prove its quality. Diminished emotion, on the other hand, will place faith's sense of God in question. With the wavering of unstable emotion, and too much sensitivity to this, there is bound to be spiritual trouble. Doubts about God's disposition toward one's soul will arise whenever dryness pervades prayer. Exaggerated spiritual presumptions, in turn, may follow emotional hours. A vexing instability is likely over the long term. When emotion is drained and God is no longer felt, the anxiety to spark passion in an unfeeling heart may be strong. The responses are surely varied and diverse. Perhaps, as Luther surmised, the felt misery of sinfulness becomes the remedy for stirring faith's passion. Religious passion can surge anew in the cry of remorse and regret. After sinning one's faith can take a passionate leap toward the saving Lord of the cross. But such a pattern hardly bespeaks a soul advancing in grace toward a deeper union with God.

~

It may be that those who seek consolation in prayer and find themselves deprived are not simply frustrated. The aridity can become not an isolated discontent, but may cut more deeply. In some cases these are souls who over time grow disappointed with God. In a certain way, it may be a spiritual vanity that has been offended in the struggle with dry prayer. Perhaps some souls consider that it is only a matter of time before God has to show approval for all their efforts. They interpret aridity wrongly and resent the sign of divine disfavor they assume it represents.

~

Sometimes souls serious about spiritual life become demanding of affection and regard from others, desirous to draw others close to themselves. It is a flaw that may have a background in a prayer life that resisted purification. The connection is not difficult to perceive. Purification in prayer is self-emptying. Long aridity if undergone with perseverance burns away our desire for satisfaction. The dryness is a humbling deprivation. But some souls cannot bear this impoverishment. When prayer has settled into chronic dryness and God shows no closeness, the response may be to seek love from others. Instead of embracing poverty, we may react by becoming possessive and demanding of human affections. It is as though we seek to secure a confirmation of being loved which the life of prayer withholds. Finding ourselves needed by others grants a spiritual worth not being received in prayer. It is good to recall that in surrendering to God, we give ourselves to a real poverty. If we make no peace with our poverty in prayer, the pursuit of consolation in human relations may strongly attract us. Without our realizing it, being needed by others placates the anxious thought that God has chosen other souls for his greater love and we have been left behind.

~

When we first begin praying, it may be thought that to desire God in prayer while feeling nothing is not possible. Yet in time a deeper stratum of desire can be discovered beneath emotion, a deeper yearning and need within our soul. We must learn to trust the existence of this hunger even before it is encountered. It is not easily known, except in the way a silent person is known when we become quiet ourselves.

$\sim$

A recognition is necessary, then, when the sensation of loving God and being loved dies away and the inner spirit is barren. Identifying emotional fervor with love for God can be hard to relinquish. Reactions vary to persistent discontent in prayer: for some people it raises doubt about the value of silent prayer and perhaps they give it up; others plod on by ponderous exertion in a discouraging tepidity; still others sense they are being humbled by God. The last response can open us to a valuable intuition—that the desire for gratification in prayer is symptomatic of an indulgent tendency still unpurified in our soul. What may seem a holy passion is a disguised desire for satisfying self. The yearning for gratification compromises prayer. It has to be mortified if we are to seek in prayer God himself.

$\sim$

Self-denial, mortification, renunciation—these have to go beyond physical concerns for sensual pleasure. There are pleasures of the spirit just as there are of the flesh. Renunciations of the former can be more daunting. As we persevere in silent prayer, a shift takes place from flesh to spirit as the primary battleground for denying self. When a dry discomfort in prayer becomes steady and unaltering, we may be tempted to force emotion out of its apparent lethargy. But there will be something false and contrived in this, and at best temporary. Every effort to insert emotion into prayer only frustrates and causes inner disturbance. Mortification is needed, but one different from any physical discipline aimed at taming a sense pleasure. In this case it is not a matter of refusing a pleasure that could be enjoyed. Instead, the aridity itself requires a renunciation. We have to dismiss it as irrelevant and unimportant. We have to let the loss of emotion pass from attention and become indifferent to the discomfort. The adjustment can provoke a fundamental change of disposition in what we seek in prayer. The self-forgetfulness this renunciation fosters opens us more fully to God's hiding in the silent deserts of prayer.

$\sim$

Emotional consolation does not have to disappear
from prayer. It is God's choice whether he wants
to grant it or not. But clearly it has to fade and
eventually cease as a *desired* gratification in prayer.
It is the longing for it that has to be burnt dry
from our soul. This has sometimes been called a
Carmelite rule of prayer. And yet often, even perhaps by them, it is little understood or accepted.
But it is deleterious to ignore this rule and to expect differently from a loving God. His love may
not coincide with our prior notions of love.

∼

We should learn as we pray longer in silence that a
dry longing for God is both inescapable and necessary. It is a necessity if we are to grow in faith, even
if the experience is at first unwelcome. This necessity has two reasons. First, our desire in prayer turns
toward someone beyond a clear grasp. Second, the
dryness conveys a truth about an encounter with
God. Aridity becomes a confirmation of God's
preference for concealment. His personal presence
will always hide from us to some degree. The aridity in a sense corroborates this choice of God's.
The link between aridity and the divine concealment educates us in the paradox of prayer. Someone draws us from a source deep in our being, and
yet gives no assurance of this. There is no tangi-

ble taste of a direct encounter, no diminishment of mystery. We come away from such prayer simply hungry and desirous. We are offering ourselves to a God of real personality.

⌇

Aridity in prayer may strengthen a concentration of love in our soul, a sign of which is a deeper calm in prayer and a detachment from emotion. Or, if not, a kind of spiritual hypochondria can take over, a concern for how one feels that must be examined constantly. The fact is that we are being given a grace to forget ourselves when we feel nothing in prayer. Unfortunately, this is often misunderstood and we may retreat into a chronic petulance in prayer, always on the verge of complaint. It may be that many who pray never realize the grace present in aridity and simply treat it as a form of mild illness, waiting stoically for a better day.

⌇

As emotion empties in prayer, silence can draw us with new attraction. The silence accompanying aridity may seem at first a vacancy, but it soon has its own taste and appeal. With more intense faith, we can accept that God hides within this silence of unfelt emotion. His presence abides in the hungers it arouses. The silence of aridity prostrates the soul, but it also incites a deeper quality of desire, distinct from former spiritual emotion. We can know the gaze of God, unseen yet trusted, because a deeper awareness rises up in the loss of felt enjoyment in prayer. The certitudes of faith exercise then a more profound impact on prayer.

~

It may seem contrary to love that we should end up unconcerned for enjoying love. Yet in prayer at least, we are capable of loving much while relishing nothing for ourselves. Love in prayer is to offer ourselves before we receive. Without that knowledge who can ever give generously to God a great love? Aridity in prayer can teach us this truth. It is meant to release our interior life from self-interest, which occurs as when we pay less attention to it. This is equally true outside prayer. The pattern is worth noting. Aridity in prayer is no obstacle to selfless actions away from prayer. Indeed it can bring a purer intention to actions which likewise have no emotion to arouse them. Emotion is unnecessary for sacrifice, for heroic charity, for hard choices. Embracing a choice purely for God's pleasure may occur more often when prayer earlier in the day suffered dissatisfaction.

~

A desire to love God, even if buried in prayer beneath a lack of feeling, is always carried outside of
prayer and draws us in ways we do not easily notice. Even when not felt, the desire for God moves
us in spontaneous, unplanned ways to actions that
would otherwise not have been attractive. The desire to love him in prayer, even in dryness, intensifies a sensitivity to a God who is never absent,
and who conceals quietly his presence when he has
found an invitation from the first hour of a day.

6

The Mind in Prayer

"Thought cannot comprehend God. And so, I prefer to abandon all I can know, choosing rather to love Him whom I cannot know. Though we cannot know Him, we can love Him. By love He may be touched and embraced, never by thought."

— *The Cloud of Unknowing*

"How is it that when there is so little time to enjoy your presence, you hide from me?"

—Saint Teresa of Avila

"These shadows are as dear to a believing heart as the lights themselves. Who would want a truth that could be assimilated at one's first contact with it, a truth that is prostituted to every kind of prying curiosity?"

—Paul Claudel

The truth we seek in prayer, in seeking God, is bound to dissatisfy our intellect. It is a necessary demand of prayer. Temporary satisfactions there are, but the one whom we

desire soon overcomes every impression of some deeper en-
try into his divine mystery. With little to enjoy in knowl-
edge, we are often left waiting in a silence whose end can-
not be anticipated. We are invited then to a holy patience
that accommodates us to our ignorance before God. With-
out this patient humility, there is no deeper adoration of
the eternal God.

Silent prayer has its well-worn rhythms of frustration and need for relief; just as our body makes its
demands for comfort after a time of deprivation.
This may be more noticeable initially in what is felt
as dryness in prayer. The emotions cannot help but
want a return to some peace and contentment when
dryness persists. But the mind, too, in prayer, has
its own sometimes piercing hungers as God hides
and becomes harder to know. He who is wholly
other than us makes himself known as more concealed, known to a greater extent as a mystery of
wounding love. And this can be the more difficult
purification in prayer.

$\sim$

The mind cannot think about God in prayer in a
way that will ensure a contact between our soul
and God. No thought in itself, even the thought
that he is looking at us with love, brings him closer.
Only a thought accompanied by a blind, passionate

desire toward God can do so. And then we are not merely thinking about God.

～

A refinement of attention is necessary if we are to seek God from a greater silence in our soul. But this cannot be simply the discipline of a mental effort. If we are to find a richer silence in prayer, it is because Jesus Christ has taken greater possession of our inner life. He has a tighter hold upon us. Attention to God in prayer is inseparable from love for him. It is because of love that we listen better in the silence of prayer. With love we wait more patiently upon his divine voice. We come to know only by love that silence is the secret language he prefers when expressing his own love for us.

～

We must strike a balance in prayer between taking up a thought about God and striving for a real encounter with God. The encounter in love is the purpose of prayer. It goes beyond what engages the mind in prayer. Unfortunately we can place a thought of God before our mind as we might lay an object of interest on a table, where it lies still and unmoving, ready for viewing. On the other hand, there are thoughts which enhance the possibility of a loving encounter with God—that God seeks our soul, that he wants to give himself, that he abandons himself to us inasmuch as he is sought. These thoughts, when pondered, cannot remain fixed and immobile, examined simply as thoughts. They urge our soul to offer itself in turn, fearless and bold before God's drawing attraction. God wants to give himself to us at this very hour. Unfailingly, this thought can enhance our own offering to God.

～

The need for recollection as a prelude to prayer contains a certain dilemma besides the difficulty of attaining it. It implies that a mental concentration is necessary if one is to pray. And so the demand to corral our wandering thoughts, to tie them down and keep them from breaching the enclosure of prayer. If we succeed in this effort, it is thought, we can presumably dwell on "spiritual things". A question arises, however, even if we manage to free our mind from distraction: how can we keep a steady focus on God, the mind taken up with the thought of someone whose mystery overcomes every thought? The stress on recollection seems to presume that in keeping our attention to prayerful thoughts, we remain in the presence of God. But perhaps God does not respond simply to an effort of attention. And perhaps neither the removal of unwelcome thoughts, nor the focus of attention, in itself, brings our soul closer to God. Far better not to think of recollection in prayer as a control of thought. Attentiveness to God is desirable in prayer. But the attention we are to cultivate comes from love, not a mental discipline directed simply at thoughts. What we should seek is a recollection that surrenders us to someone entirely beyond our thought, a beloved who will never stop to rest for long within a particular thought.

∼

It is remarkable how demanding some thoughts are for a show of interest in an hour of prayer. Many times these are useless thoughts, not worth much trouble even outside prayer. But they seem to take our desire for silence as an invitation to compete with God, and often they win. But can there be something else in this difficulty to turn toward God in prayer? Does the appeal, at times, of a trivial distraction give evidence of the need for a certain humility about ourselves? We would like to keep our thoughts exclusively on God in prayer. But we cannot think of him so readily. Perhaps no particular thought about God can bring for long a consistent calming effect to the mind. At times we can simply desire him without knowing him so well, hoping that this desire will plunge us into a deeper silence and more intense love. Unfortunately the noise may continue to intrude. For long stretches in prayer, we sometimes can do nothing better than reach out in a blind gaze toward God, trying to ignore the sounds that surround us.

~

A silence in prayer that leaves our soul ill at ease may be a sign that we must search more intently for God's will. The discomfort may be hiding a divine request, a question not yet heard, requiring an effort to discover it. But it is rather easy to refuse this difficult silence and its uncertainty. It is possible to close our ear to God when he is addressing us. We can adopt a forced self-assurance, convinced that everything God wants we have already given. But with that thought the deeper and richer silence available in prayer may become more uninhabitable. We will be pulled to the surface like a diver in water who must come up for air.

~

We have not taken up in prayer a work that can be mastered. The notion of a successful practitioner is out of place. Indeed, prayer is not a work at all. Efficiency in its practice is a contradiction to its truth as a sacred companionship. It may require discipline, commitment, renunciations. But essentially it is a return again and again in love to someone known more deeply over time. It is a turn to a mysterious personal presence without expectation of what will be received. Familiarity with God even as he hides demands a trust in the permanency of this friendship. Sometimes that means a search for him; other times a relaxation with him. Love alone determines how much we realize over time the privilege of this unequal friendship.

~

There may be souls of spiritual depth who presume in themselves a meager capacity for prayer because they find interior silence unachievable. They desire more than anything a peaceful recollection alone with God and instead experience frequent disturbance of their thoughts in prayer. They are quite mistaken, sometimes, about their lack of deeper prayer. It may even be that God prefers it this way. The manner in which people and events from outside prayer cling to their thoughts is actually matched by an intense undercurrent of desire cleaving to God during times of prayer and extending beyond prayer. This dominant desire for God operates beneath the turbulence of distraction. It is the primary spiritual orientation of the person. Their mental activity may seem caught up in haphazard thoughts, but there is nonetheless a steady flow of desire for God. This provides a deeper layer of loving contact between God and the soul even if the person seems to enjoy no satisfaction. Their union with God in prayer is a concealed one, hidden from their own perception. This quality of hiddenness may be most salutary for the subsequent generosity of such souls. Sometimes these are souls who have been given a poor and obscure role in the divine plan for the salvation of other souls. Their experience in prayer is consistent with the holy poverty of their lives.

∼

We believe in a God who spoke human words with a human voice. There are souls, on the other hand, who sometimes imagine they have entered a mystical dark night when actually they have stopped listening to the voice of Our Lord speaking from the gospel pages. They have forgotten that Jesus can speak to us with the same words that he first used long ago. When there is a darkness in prayer and God seems silent, Jesus' words must be heard again: "What are you looking for? Will you lay down your life for me? Have I been with you all this time, and still you do not know me?" A living voice is speaking in these questions, a voice layered in tones of divine enigma, yet often direct in his personal invitation. His questions, in particular, invite us as a bridge summons a weary traveler. They beckon us to walk across into the mystery of his divine presence.

～

Christian meditation as traditionally taught required an exercise in discursive thought. The mind engaged in a sustained reflection, usually on a subject taken from the life of Christ in the gospel. The effort was to ponder, search for insight, seek out spiritual implications in gospel passages, settle on resolutions for one's personal life. For many people it may have been that the primary benefit was to enhance the pursuit of virtue outside prayer. Clarity in one's resolutions for virtue is a constant refrain in the method. But did such prayer place a soul nakedly in the truth of its absolute need for God? Did it foster the patience to bear God's concealment in silence and emptiness? In prayer it may be more important to encounter what cannot be done, what cannot be resolved on, except by a work that is directed from God's hand. Sometimes we forget how little we can do on our own—in prayer or outside the time of prayer.

～

The recommendation not to think many thoughts in prayer, not to speak many words, would have

more worth if it were not at times impossible.
On the other hand, to accept as the will of God
the prayer given on a particular day, whether it
be dry, distracted, or serene and insightful, shows
a healthy realization that prayer is not a pursuit
of efficiency and success. There are difficulties in
prayer, and suggestions are sometimes valuable to
counter them. But they can never be proposed as
precise solutions guaranteed to overcome struggles
in prayer. Repeating an ejaculation, for instance, or
gazing on a crucifix, or returning to a single verse of
Scripture—these practical suggestions are all useful. But they imply above all a need for simplicity
in prayer. What we can forget is the importance
of extending that simplicity always to our interior
longing for God. What God desires is our deeper
receptivity. He seeks that our Fiat to him become
a more constant disposition in prayer. Sometimes
in the churning waters of prayer we overlook what
gives prayer its true anchor and steadiness.

∼

It is of course not necessary to banish insights from
prayer, which would be foolish, but rather to experience their value as a stimulus to love. Any insights gained in prayer are meant to provoke deeper
desires of soul. If they do not intensify the desire

to love, they stop short of their purpose. Indeed, love for Jesus Christ ought to conclude every effort to think about God. A reflection on God has no proper finality unless it urges us to love the mystery of the incarnate Son of God, who in turn invites us to surrender and offer ourselves to him in a quite personal manner precisely at the juncture in which all thought exhausts itself and ceases.

～

To take up a position on a hillside for viewing an impressive sunset on the horizon is quite different from leaving our place to seek for a better angle of view and missing the most radiant colors of the sun going down. This is what happens sometimes in the life of prayer when we are anxious for satisfactions in our thoughts of God or in our meditations.

～

The words of Jesus in the gospel must never become so familiar that we dispense with pondering them in prayer. We must not let happen what sometimes happens when people leave their native home for a foreign land and never return, forgetting after a time the favorite words of their childhood.

～

The intellect and will in prayer do not remain in an easy harmony. There is a tension in the satisfactions possible to each. Our intellect can take hold of a fresh thought, some insight into Scripture or a theological idea, and find satisfaction. The will in prayer cannot be appeased so readily; nothing partial satiates it. The will can never be really content as long as God remains unpossessed. This tension poses a dilemma. If we halt at the intellect's satisfactions, this may leave our soul's deeper desire for God unmoved. The fact is that every thought we pursue in prayer is at best a distant glimpse toward a truth we do not yet fully see. There can be thoughts about God in prayer, or an absence of thoughts, but in either case the intellect's primary "usefulness" in prayer is when it exercises a blind certitude of intense faith. This becomes a conduit, as it were, for being drawn to a more intense love for God. Our thought must learn over time to enjoy less in prayer and to embrace darkness without protest, remembering that every silencing of thought invites a humbling of the mind. Only perhaps in a deeper humility of intellect does our will choose for God with greater purity and love.

~

The closer we draw to God, the less any particular conception of God aids the life of prayer. Yet certain thoughts do stimulate our soul and at times spark a release from some weariness in prayer: to recall, for instance, that Jesus Christ from the cross at Calvary casts his eyes upon the entirety of our life at this very moment; or that all times of trial are passing, including the current condition of what may seem a poor prayer; or that Jesus has turned to us always whenever we plunged more deeply into need and poverty. These pondering thoughts can be chosen, and the result is often a return to God in greater confidence.

～

We initiate a time of prayer sensibly when we prostrate ourselves before God in adoration. We bow in adoration because of two truths—our own nothingness and God's infinite goodness. The act of adoring God prepares our soul for the God who remains hidden always even as we meet him. His concealment is a presence encountered best in our own prostration. If we lift our eyes too quickly for him, we miss this mysterious concealed proximity. We know his presence with greater certainty with our face plunged to the ground. The prostration submits our soul's desire to God. Our eyes, now full of dust, are ready to look blindly in desire toward God alone.

～

Adoration is a richer use of intellect in prayer than a discursive meditation, even the most insightful meditation, precisely because it brings poverty to the soul. It makes us poor by stretching us toward the eternity in God. It inclines us to be silent before a divine gaze that no particular hour possesses as its own. Done best in silence and without thoughts, when our mind is humbled before God's inaccessibility to the effort of thought, adoration places our being before the infinite being of God's goodness. A profound experiential truth is realized. God in his goodness is the unnamable "I Aм". We, in our naked nothingness—we are not.

7

Aberrations

"It is absolutely necessary to shun as the most pernicious of vices the reflex action of the mind, the tendency to come back on ourselves. . . . This absence of any return on oneself, this very pure desire of God alone, is the essential condition of contemplation."

—Jacques Maritain

"There are souls who seek solitude merely in order to find themselves: there are others who seek it so that they may give themselves."

—Augustín Guillerand

"One keeps forgetting to go right down to the foundations. One doesn't put the question marks *deep* enough down."

—Ludwig Wittgenstein

A quiet aberration has been present in the Church for some time: the quest for God disconnected from the doctrinal tradition of Catholic faith; souls moved by a religious impulse for God, but captivated by more esoteric mystical possibilities; the core beliefs of Christianity not abandoned in an overt or hostile manner, but shunted aside, supplanted by aspirations for an experiential touch or taste of God. Variations of this kind arose as the dogmatic truths of Christianity received less attention in public catechesis. Stress on an immanent God accessible to religious experience replaced a proper awareness of the exalted transcendence of God's nature. In a time of doctrinal confusion, the doors of the divine hiding place seemed to open wide and invite an easy entry.

A shift has been taking place in the motive behind religious seeking. The desire for "spirituality" rather than a need to know ultimate truth often draws the religious seeker. But by this is meant a search for inward "experiences of God", which entice as a superior form of truth. If they can be had, it is thought, they will convey the essence of religious truth, rather than an assent in faith to Christian revelation. The danger is a kind of quasi-Christianity taking shape which may retain portions of the Christian proclamation, but which also strays into excesses and distortions. The errors come as the boundary between subjective interiority and the reality of God becomes soft and porous, so much so that this boundary breaks down and the two become indistinguishable. In more radical expressions of this tendency, there is no truth of God apart from an experience of him within oneself. A soul knows him inasmuch as it inwardly experiences him. The inward experience alone confirms religious truth. Unfortunately the claim to be experientially touched by God may have no basis in reality. But realizing the error becomes more difficult as so-called experiences of God are valued and sought. The elevation of private experiences of God to a form of truth preempts every objection to the genuineness of an actual contact with the divine.

~

Catholic doctrinal truth and sound spirituality are companions. They support and protect each other; they shed luminosity on the importance of the other. But they also starve together when either is neglected, when one does not nourish the other. Their mutual need demands at various times in personal lives and in the Church their simultaneous recovery. The mutual dependency of doctrine and spirituality has been evident in a negative manner in the recent decades, as the downward drift of catechesis in the Church became more widespread. This should have been foreseen, that a loss of care in the teaching of divine mysteries would have repercussions on how souls perceive a relationship with God. Some proposed that a clearing away of abstract notions about God would open the way to more immediate experiences of God. But that expectation proved illusory. With the loss of clarity and repetition in the pedagogy of Catholic doctrine, confusion in spirituality began to spread. This did not require that dogmatic truths were rejected, only that they were ignored. With doctrinal truth a more peripheral concern, a private search for God became for many people more attractive. The claim of extraordinary religious experiences was more often heard. Without roots in revealed truths, souls moved by a hunger for God sometimes became itinerant wanderers in the shadows and clouds of religious seeking.

～

In the more esoteric instances of pursuing experiences of God, the labyrinth of the soul's interiority is the temple where the religious seeker must make pilgrimage. The passage is no simple journey. To traverse it requires a training in the rigors of interior silence. Learning to overcome an undisciplined mind is necessary, and thus arises the special interest in Asian methods of silencing the mind. They are adopted to tame the impulses of thought and so convey a soul through the holy layers of quietude dormant within selfhood. Within the caverns of inner consciousness await fertile encounters with God. The one condition is that a soul navigate this passage on the currents of a pure silence. All thought must be at rest and extinguished. At the end of that journey into the soul's deeper silence, the hiding place of God may emerge, a garden within the soul's inner recesses, the coveted sanctuary where we presumably meet the mystery of God.

～

The popular appeal of methods of prayer using a mantra raises some questions in this regard. These methods propose a silent repetition in the mind of a single word known as a mantra, steadily and rhythmically repeated in the manner that breathing itself has a rhythm. At the same time a person practices an inattention to particular thoughts that arise during the prayer, letting them fade from view. The inattention to passing thought is not by force of will, as though one had to conquer by mental effort the recurrence of unwelcome distractions. The slow, inward repeating of the mantra in itself releases the mind from intrusive thoughts and their veneer of importance. By repeating the mantra, particular thoughts that might draw interest drift away before disappearing from sight. As the method is used and the clearing away of thoughts becomes a regular exercise, a bare and naked state of mind can be achieved more consistently. Consciousness arrives habitually at an open, inward space, accessible now, it is thought, to the presence of God residing at the center of the soul. A tranquillity felt at the center of that inward emptiness seems to confirm that God is drawing the soul to himself.

~

The method, it is said, shows immediate benefits: it is a way of bringing silence to the mind, of easing anxiety and nervous strain, of relaxing the whole being of a person. As the practice continues, the sustained rhythm of repeating a single word soothes consciousness, infusing it with a mood, a feeling of peace and harmony within itself. Consciousness, in effect, simplifies with the repetition of a mantra; it becomes free and unencumbered. Instead of discursive meanderings of thought, a simple state of attention without thoughts more often fills the mind. Ideally, silence permeates one's inner being in a complete manner, so that no thought competes with the slowly repeating rhythm of the mantra. The mantra after a time repeats itself without effort. Consciousness becomes like a boat at anchor rocking in peaceful waves.

~

The exercise is directed at the achievement of this inner tranquillity, and not simply at emptying thought, because God is assumed to be present in that peace, and the source of it. With the mind free of thought, unfocused except for the slow repetition of the mantra, and the inner spirit serene and enjoying a tangible peace, it would seem that God is laying a gentle hand upon the soul, pleased with it, inviting a plunge into further depths where he awaits encounter. The soul has only to give itself to this inward peace. The method seems reliable, the gains consistent and real. Inner tranquillity, the release from stress, coincides with perseverance in method. The peace, it is said, confirms the presence of God. On the other hand, one should note that consciousness can be pacified in many ways, by listening to the rush of waves on a beach, to the leaves in the woods in an autumn wind, or to rainfall on the roof of a summer cabin. These are not equivalent to the voice of God speaking to a soul. They are God's creations, and reasons one might turn a thought to God. But the peace they bring is a natural effect, not identifiable in itself with an action of grace.

∼

The objection that caution be exercised, that illusions are possible, may appear contrary to evidence. Nonetheless to assume that the soul is experiencing God in its felt tranquillity, that God's presence necessarily accompanies the peace enjoyed in the prayer, neglects another possibility. The benefits may be the result of natural psychological operations. The inner quiet and serenity can be a natural effect of repeating the mantra. Controlled experiments have shown that the mental repetition of a single word for a half-hour relaxes the mind and empties it of thought, producing the same effects on blood pressure and heartbeat achieved in hypnosis by holding a subject's concentrated gaze on the rhythmic movement of an object swinging slowly in front of the eyes. In both cases a profound relaxation permeates the psyche. Thoughts fade gently away and soon the mind enjoys a state of silence. With nothing to trouble awareness, the feeling of inner peacefulness becomes itself the focus of attention.

~

What, then, is happening spiritually by using a mantra in this manner? While at first appearing to enrich a personal relationship with God, the method may simply isolate consciousness within itself. The thought of self may seem to diminish as thoughts drift away and their demand for attention weakens. But in emptying one's mental operation, there is no necessary sequel of grace. It does not follow that God blesses this state of inward emptiness. What seems to be a release *from* self may actually be a plunge *into* self—consciousness drawing in upon itself, turning reflexively on its own operation, watchful of its own inner experience. Rather than an experience of God, the peace that permeates consciousness may be a more intense experience of self. It may be simply the self that is passively enjoyed in the soothing tranquillity generated by the mantra's repetition. If so, God may not be "there" at all in the experience of inward peace. Diving down into the depths of a peaceful silence within inner consciousness is not to encounter the living God, but rather to enclose oneself in the self-absorption of a fallacious peace.

～

A type of spiritual Pelagianism may be operating here. The error of the ancient Pelagians was to presume a strength in human nature for the perfection of virtue, with no need for grace. In their view we are capable of holiness without God's help, of spiritual fruitfulness apart from grace. In the self-reliance adopted by a Pelagian spirituality, it is we ourselves who stoke the flames of virtue, while perhaps God looks on admiring the achievement. This amounts to an "attitudinal heresy", a failure of humble recognition that we depend on God for any greater goodness. Variations of this error occur when recourse to divine assistance is considered unnecessary or at least minimized, or when we think our own action somehow incites grace into our lives. The possibility is strong for such a mistake when prayer methods are identified as a means to a contemplative encounter with God. One takes up a method of prayer in expectation of an inner experience. After some practice the inner experience is enjoyed with consistent regularity. As long as the method is used, the inward experience returns with predictable success. The method seems to assure continuation. Indeed, to all appearances it might seem that the method serves as a catalyst to grace. The grace can be expected to continue on the condition that one is faithful to the method of prayer. But, unfortunately, there may be little grace actually at work.

~

There is a common thread in false spiritual pursuits. God's transcendence, his infinite otherness, is increasingly lost from sight, replaced by a conviction of God *tangibly* present within one's own soul. The veil of divine concealment purportedly lifts. The soul enjoys in direct ways a God who now unites himself to the soul. The silence and peace inhabiting the soul are indistinguishable from God's own presence. In a certain sense this is to make the features of mysticism a measure of spirituality. The esoteric becomes the norm. The rare and ineffable become a coveted goal. But what if this is incorrect and God in himself, as Saint John of the Cross remarks, is incomprehensible and inaccessible to our inward experience? Catholic spiritual tradition affirms that God is by his nature wholly other to our being and therefore uncontainable, unencloseable, within any spiritual experience. We do not take hold of him at the center of our soul even as he is present there.

～

As the prospect of directly experiencing God tantalizes and sparks at times an infatuation with mysticism, the more subdued invitation of the gospel to die to self in service to others is often ignored. The impulse toward humble charity gradually weakens. A self-referential habit will be more evident in a life, which reflects the self-absorption that false types of prayer foster. The irony should not be missed. One can end up living less generously the life of charity as an aspiration to some form of spurious possession of God dominates one's religious pursuit.

～

All deeper prayer depends in part on a release from tendencies to egoism. The prerogative of an "I" in control of experience must give way, even disappear. The search for God in prayer has no use for this "I" interpreting experience. On the other hand, no kind of method or particular practice in prayer is available to relinquish the "I". A method would be another effort of control. It is enough simply that we become poor in turning toward God, casting aside every possessive urge. Every impulse to conquer God even with love is too often a surging up of egoism once again. It is only an impoverishing love in prayer that allows the "I" to disappear, a love inattentive to self, empty of self, conquered by another. All deeper prayer demands this impoverishment of the "I", a poverty that has no conclusion, no boundary crossed that would return the "I" in some richer manner.

~

The hidden God abides in our inmost spirit. This is the great contemplative truth. But notable stress is laid on the truth of concealment in this presence of God within our soul. It is a companionship which may give us no *tangible* assurance and is never predictably possessed. He is certainly with us and in faith we know his presence, approachable at the inmost core of our being where our own existence ends and another is present. Contemplation, moved by love and blind certitude, seeks this one who is completely other, who will never be sufficiently known even while offering certainty of his presence. The paradox of intimacy with God is constant and intensifies: a blind ignorance accompanies every deeper companionship with God; his near proximity in love is never without the hovering shadows of darkness.

∼

The question whether God is experienced in prayer may seem unanswerable. How do we know? Is there some way to measure within the experience itself? Perhaps not, but there is the traditional test of fruitful prayer, observable in the urge to self-giving when prayer is concluded. Generosity toward others upon leaving prayer, a soul turned humbly and charitably toward others, a tendency to self-effacement, these are among the reliable signs of graces given during prayer. If a soul has loved God during a time of prayer, the same love requires becoming a servant to the needs of others outside of prayer.

8

Poverty of Soul

"At the time of prayer, we should allow the soul undisturbed rest and put all our knowledge off to the side. . . . What he wants is for the soul to behave like a fool—which is just what it is in his presence. And he is so humble himself that despite all our wretchedness he is willing to keep us beside him."

—Saint Teresa of Avila

"Since I have rooted myself in nothing, I find that nothing is lacking to me."

—Saint John of the Cross

"When we pray, we are all God's beggars."

—Saint Augustine

There is a lifetime mystery in the poverty God sees in our soul that parallels our incomprehension toward the divine mystery. This poverty, no matter what our external life shows, does not at some point clearly expose itself. It cannot be sought as an item of self-knowledge. It retains always an unknown, elusive quality. At best it is partially

*experienced as a secret truth known to God. We brush up
against it not so much in gains and discoveries but in every
loss that takes something precious or important from our
life. Poverty has a way of becoming one with our soul.
Even hidden from our view we can come to know over a
lifetime that this poverty is what God loves most in our
soul.*

There must be a way of entering in prayer into our
true nothingness without God. But what is this
poverty in ourselves that must accompany prayer,
especially at the outset? It cannot be simply a
thought of our unworthiness before God. Much
less can it be a mood of despondency about self.
We must forget ourselves in prayer if we are to
turn our desire more fully toward God. We do not
leave the self behind by dwelling on our wretchedness. An absence of thought for self suggests a better response. But this cannot be sought in itself as
the goal of prayer. Simply emptying our mind of
thoughts does not mean we turn ourselves to God.
If we forget self in prayer, it is because we want
God and nothing but him. Only in desiring God
more intently do we become more silent toward
ourselves, more insignificant, poorer before God.

∼

Poverty of soul cannot be a matter for labored reflection. We do not need to investigate or analyze

our poverty. Such an effort would be like trying to probe the desires our soul experiences toward God in prayer. Rather, our internal poverty of soul hinges on our absolute dependency on God. It is a recognition of our incapacity for God unless he draws us. We are not freed from ourselves unless released by another hand. But this freedom is not a desperate venture we can hardly expect to occur. Our nothingness attracts God's love in the way a poor child's smile draws our own emotion.

∼

It is possible that sometimes we proclaim our unworthiness before God at the same time that we resent what seems to be God's lack of concern for our soul. Our sense of unworthiness is to a degree contrived, a borrowed notion expected of a soul seeking God, without deeper truth. There may be something of a humble posture in our prayer, but there is also a basic complaint. We may not articulate the thought in an explicit manner, but perhaps we believe that our spiritual efforts imply certain rights and privileges with God. While beating our breasts in a back pew, our deeper conviction may be that we deserve better from God, more attention for all our striving.

∼

That a soul should suffer by wondering whether it has any importance to God might seem a useless anxiety, a form of spiritual egoism. Why should anyone expect special attention from God? Does not humility demand accepting our insignificance? Yet surely a conviction of being favored by God contributed to the making of saints. Their desire for God intensified as they realized they were known tenderly by God. They passed through dark uncertainties, but they returned always to his gaze on their lives. At some point they grasped the lofty truth that God's favor includes the gift of saturating a life with greater poverty.

~

A deeper love for God is inseparable from being wounded over time. Only by a divine wound does our love for God intensify. This is in part a wound of inner discontent within our soul, the powerlessness of never giving ourselves adequately to love. Over a lifetime we may find that it is not healed with more love. Every increase of love only magnifies a demand to love more. Whenever God draws from us a deeper longing for himself, we should expect this wound will be felt. There is something of a strange consequence to this. We realize better the insufficiency of our love whenever God draws closer to our soul. Nearer to God, we become poorer.

~

It is the nature of love to undergo impoverishment. When we find this baffling, our thought should turn to Jesus Christ. The link of love and impoverishment is sublime in Jesus. God's way of showing his unfathomable love was to take our flesh and embrace the hardship and death of a poor man's existence. Indeed what in a human life can claim exclusion from God asking that it be offered back to him? Deeper relations with God imply a readiness to lose everything, to have everything taken from us, no longer protected from even human love departing from our lives. Perhaps there is no significant taste of poverty until a soul experiences that its sole companions in the current hour have become heavenly persons it does not see.

~

Before he gives himself more fully God surely waits for the hunger of a soul to reach a depth of intensity. The soul's pleading must begin to resemble a beggar's voice long accustomed to refusal. For God it may be the wait of a human lifetime before he hears this tone rising up from the soul. Yet it can be sooner if one day our soul is aware it has nothing to offer God of its own possession. Indeed sooner still if we realize that the emptiness and poverty we feel internally is the gift we must sacrifice now to him. Then surely God will be patient no longer. He will not delay, but draw quickly near.

~

It is impossible that poverty of spirit is learned in fast and easy lessons. No natural disposition exists for it. Only providentially, often by events that unmask a deeper loneliness in a soul, can impoverishment ever be welcomed and even become attractive. Perhaps it does so only then because God is recognized in a new manner, gentle in his touch, incapable of crushing what is poor.

~

There can be spiritual nights in prayer when our soul feels unable to find its voice, or at least a voice that used to speak freely with God. The effort to converse with God may seem to attract no divine interest. Our words may seem to draw only a silent response. The thought can occur of being a stranger to God. We may even feel an attraction in that prospect. Perhaps God might take notice again if he realizes he has to pursue us as he did in an earlier time. But of course this thought is foolish and wrong. It is one thing to feel lost and alone. It is another to imagine that however abject and poor we become, we can ever disappear from his gaze of love.

~

The anxious thought of a day to come, with its hypothetical possibilities, can always return to trouble a time of prayer. And then we may find ourselves glancing down at waters into which we seemed to step shortly before with fearless abandon. This hesitation, too, must be passed through on the way to greater interior poverty.

~

If we find ourselves in a malaise with God we do well to seek the company of a tabernacle. Those who know God more deeply come to know a recurring attraction for him in the Eucharist. They come to know as well their own poverty while praying before the Eucharist. His disguised appearance in the Sacrament lifts the cover of poverty from their own soul. In the presence of his poverty, their own poverty no longer intimidates. They sense intuitively that it draws and even seduces his love.

~

Greater faith does not shield us from a poverty in our belief. A deeper faith is not to enjoy a security that no thought can upset. On the contrary, fears and vague whispers can languish at times within us, as if without our notice an unknown intruder had violated the inner sanctuary of our soul. A dark question may begin to rise up from silence which disappears before anything more is heard. If we sometimes suffer occasions of shadow and doubt, it is best to pay them no mind. There is little perhaps we can do to keep them from returning. This is a time to discover again a humble need for God at the poorest depth of the soul, our heart clasping him as a companion not to be forsaken.

~

Restless thoughts cascading down barren slopes, the soul cut off from inner calm, the heart carried off on a rivulet toward dry sand—if we seek an explanation for difficulties in prayer, we may be wasting time. These trials, whatever their cause, require an attitude of humble perseverance. The perseverance in turn enlightens us to the need of becoming poorer. It is only in true indigence that we appreciate the value of leaving ourselves with no option but to offer all in our life to God.

~

The mystics sometimes describe rare hours when appearances lift their mask momentarily, revealing a harmony within all things which descends as well into the soul, leaving behind a great longing. And perhaps such experiences can be ours also in a milder way if we rest our thoughts in God and embrace a certainty that all events have their divine reason beyond the reach of our human heart. But these felt certitudes, too, are often temporary and depart with a loss. Afterward we may find our eyes returning to shadows, wishing for light and a comprehension that might be permanent and crush every dark question. Perhaps we must simply accept that being poor is no obstacle to our companionship with God. Our relations with God are not tied to any transient experience, for better or for worse.

~

Poverty may first enter our lives only by accepting our insignificance in the setting in which we live. We ought to observe the workings of divine providence in this regard. Any experience of being left alone, disregarded, forgotten—if it does not isolate the soul and make it retreat inwardly—invites a recognition. Our unimportance to others can combine with a fruitful realization. The more we disappear from the attention of others, the more we are watched by God in a different manner.

~

A purer love for God has always this trait: that it has become a poorer love. It offers nothing to enhance an external self taken up with activity. It makes everything at the surface of personality seem insubstantial and discardable, to be exchanged for a deeper truth not passing away. We may notice a pattern in this. The desire to love God expressed in prayer implies concrete actions meant to complete it. But when our actions are chosen later, they may be far less bold than the earlier prayer. Desires may seem to dissipate once we are outside prayer and now face actual choices. Our actions are flawed and seem even to mock the earlier desire in prayer to give ourselves all to God. It is as though this desire for God, sincere in the dark quiet of prayer, cannot withstand the harsh light of our feeble character. Our soul can seem false, caught in illusions. The discrepancy between desire and actions seems painfully clear. Returning to prayer, we may reproach ourselves with doubts—was the earlier prayer pretentious, a vain posturing before God? Yet all this is perhaps not a sign of a counterfeit aspiration. It is a taste of our powerlessness to love except as a gift from God. Our incapacity for deeper love without divine help remains throughout a lifetime. We simply experience it more keenly in our actions than in our prayer.

~

Sometimes, perhaps, we might wish for a kind of proficiency in spiritual poverty, not realizing the contradiction in this desire. The need to become poor is a great spiritual demand. Unlike exterior virtues, however, spiritual poverty will never be granted to us if we seek the satisfaction of becoming more capable in a practice of it.

～

The encounter in prayer with God's hiding has many ways to make us poor. There may be an inward conviction, for example, that God is asking something of us. But we are unable to identify what this might be. Every effort to know is unavailing. The effort ends in futility, and we find ourselves confused and interiorly poor. It can be like hearing the words of a foreign language spoken in barely audible tones. We want to get closer and recognize at least some word. But nothing of meaning reaches our ear. The lack of recognition frustrates. Yet with God it is best sometimes not to expect a clear recognition. He may often choose to touch our desire alone in prayer without leaving behind any familiar words.

～

The awareness of incompletion, of a task unfinished in life, still awaiting discovery, may not bring peace to our heart. Yet we should not evade this recognition. With it we aspire to give more. Indeed one of the memorable moments of prayer may come when Jesus' question—"What is it you ask of me?"—slips unexpectedly into our heart and we are dumbfounded what to answer, stunned at Jesus addressing himself directly to us, knowing that our previous answer has always avoided a greater gift of ourselves.

~

There is perhaps an answer that God awaits. "Father, I abandon myself in your hands. Do with me as you will. . . . I am ready for all, I accept all." A prayer of abandonment to God, as in the prayer composed by Charles de Foucauld, cannot be prayed except from a deeper poverty of soul. A spirit of abandonment is to relinquish autonomy, to sacrifice a right of determination over our future, to mortify the impulse to forecast or predict. It is to offer our subsequent days blindly to God, to leave what is to come entirely to God's choice. In short, it is to become poor. This divestment of ourselves is surely a necessary condition for a surrender to God that does not fall back on a confidence in our own power to give our lives to him. It cannot take place without an implicit promise not to question God at a later day in order that he might reconsider his will. In the absence of any knowledge of what God may do with such an open permission, this prayer repeated over a lifetime can be a form of slow dying, which in God's plan is no doubt what it is meant to accomplish. It is made easier if we realize that giving up control over the remaining days of our life can only lead to happiness.

9

Sacrifice and Self-denial

"In the exercise of this self-denial everything else, and even more, is discovered and accomplished. If one fails in this exercise, the root and sum of all the virtues, the other methods would amount to no more than going about in circles."

—Saint John of the Cross

"Don't you see that you have lost what you did not give?"

—Saint Augustine

"When one desires nothing, one will have all one needs."

—Saint Bernadette

Once the hiddenness of God is adequately realized, a new impulse is felt in the spiritual life. The concealment of God implies his actual presence in hiding. Although unseen, he remains near and approachable, an observer and companion, one who may be touched invisibly with love. This realization opens a soul to the value of sacrifice as an expression of love. The experience of deprivation in interior prayer compels a soul to seek a parallel form of self-emptying in sacrifice and renunciation. It is a way of contact with the hiddenness of God. Faith inclines us toward losing self as a means of touching the hidden heart of God.

"Unless a grain of wheat falls into the earth and dies . . ." (Jn 12:24). Self-renunciation as the gospel proposes it cannot be equated simply with the ascetical disciplines adopted by monks and heroic souls. Then it is easily dismissed as either a negation of life's joys for those so grimly inclined or as an excessive challenge that only saints can manage. Saintly lives, if examined with care, do show a profound capacity for self-renunciation, but only the surface of this is ascetical practice. A life like Mother Teresa's, for example, was filled with daily ascetical choices. But from the posthumous revelations of her beatification process we know now that the deeper renunciations of her life came in persevering in love through a sustained interior darkness she suffered over many years. This latter trial was a self-renunciation that plunged far beneath physical mortifications. Her passion for sacrifice reached down to a profound spiritual dying to self. It is evidence, perhaps, of a constant provocation caused by the concealment of God to a soul intense with love. The hidden God draws from such a soul great desires for hidden immolations unseen by others.

The visible generosities in such a life are a sign of this deeper renunciation of the interior spirit.

⁓

Should a passion for God subsume all other desires in a life? This would imply that everything we love in life other than God somehow competes with God, even steals from God the love that should be all his. This notion is incompatible with the tender affections for particular human lives that was present in saints. Their passion for God did not make them passionless toward the world they lived in. They had a cleaving attachment to God, but it did not extinguish friendship in their lives. They never became indifferent to human love. Rather, a refinement rooted in supernatural passion affected their love for human persons. Their great passion for God made every human love like the swell of a wave riding upon a powerful ocean undercurrent.

⁓

Sacrifice and renunciation demand hard choices. But how is it that they lead to greater love? An attraction must accompany costly choices, without which there is no real love in them. This appeal is to realize that God delights in sacrificial love. The thought of giving pleasure to God can sweep away a hesitation and reluctance in facing difficult choices. More intense acts of this kind are chosen for love of a God who in hiding secretly rejoices in them. This is not a sentimentality toward God, but a most sober faith. Many souls, unfortunately, think only of self-inflicted pain in the sacrifices they undertake. They do not lift their eyes to the face of Christ on the cross and its mysterious awareness. If they did so, they might be overwhelmed by his eyes gazing kindly on their efforts to share, at least in some small part, his time of terrible suffering.

～

Spirituality is never equivalent to an advancement in willpower, akin to a muscular development of soul. Yet a great deal does depend on a strong will. The quality of will in a person often divides those who settle for less from those who give themselves more fully to God. We depend on grace, true, but all is not grace alone. Choices undertaken with vigor and courage are decisive. Beneath these choices must be a stubborn determination for God, an intransigence of spirit not to turn back from the path to God. But how does this passion for God take hold except in learning to deny our weaker needs and inclinations? Some of this is learned in the struggle with temptation and sin. But of course God asks more from us than a virtuous avoidance of sin. If we want to love God with intensity, we must be ready as well to offer everything he may eventually take from us. We can expect there are unknown renunciations awaiting us that make the refusal of any temptation a mere practice run for the main event still to come. This prospect is much easier to accept when we realize that God will never take anything from us without giving himself in the exchange.

∼

Asceticism is no measure of a soul. Nonetheless people who acquire a taste for mortification are less likely to halt when difficult interior purifications commence. The perseverance in later trials is linked to a quality of soul developed earlier. It is not just that practices of self-denial and sacrifice develop a strong will. These earlier renunciations also carve a deeper sincerity into the soul, a determination to seek God at all cost. They accustom a soul to God's hidden presence encouraging every effort of generosity. They allow a soul to trust God even in weariness and fatigue. All this can be decisive when God begins to show us how poor we really are despite every exercise of our will.

∼

Self-renunciation can be an imposing demand. We can tire of what seems to be its persistent bidding.

Those like Saint John of the Cross who insist on
it, however, were also sensitive to how adept God
is at hiding himself. Implicit in this saint's ascetical
proposals is a question whether our desire for a
God who hides himself the more he is sought can
survive long while keeping company with unworthy rivals to his love.

~

No one perceives the value of a spirit of mortification in prayer who has not learned to deny common pleasures to the physical senses. This, too, is
a clear teaching of Saint John of the Cross. The
link between indulgent tendencies in one's bodily
life and those in the interior realm of spiritual gratification is a parallel demand for mortification. It
may be foreign to our ears today on both counts.
But Saint John of the Cross is sharp in his warning: no soul is given deeper graces in prayer while
disdaining exterior or interior austerity.

~

Dying to self in any mortification does not leave
the interior spirit drowning in nothingness, empty
of substance. In refusing what could be indulged,
we do not disappear. It is not as though without
select enjoyments we become ghostly or inhuman.
On the contrary a release from a shallow self takes

place in every act of self-denial—a new manner of self-possession. A desire for God can fill the space where an unnecessary satisfaction might have been sought. A deeper passion for God can burn where we might have lit a brief flame that soon turned dark in our soul.

~

Vitality of soul is inseparable from a spirit of detachment that love produces. As love increases, so, too, does a release from proprietary interests and possessive needs. The result is the lightness of an unburdened soul. The energy in action of saintly lives was a sign of this freedom of love when a soul acquires greater purity in its desires. Yet more than self-denials are required for the detachment that accompanies a more intense love for God. Renunciations mean little without a hunger for God that proves less manageable, less subject to control, as a life continues. The soul of every saint was selfless and generous because the pursuit of God had conquered its inmost desire.

~

Sometimes people are forceful and aggressive in the very good they do, as if pressed by a deadline, driven by a need to perform. But they do not enjoy the good they do for others. No doubt it goads them privately that they are left dissatisfied, as though they were constantly losing a competition with themselves. Unfortunately, it is a symptom of missing the concealed presence of God. He wants our goodness to bring us joy and delight precisely because it is his delight to compel it.

∼

A rich man might give away a sizable sum of money from his pocket to the nearest beggar he passes, and feel happy about it. On the other hand, he is unlikely to give up a keepsake of sentimental value if it is directly requested. And no one would fault him for the refusal. In a similar way, it is often easier to renounce possessions than to surrender to God human attachments or a need to be loved. The experience of sacrifice can be like this. It is easier to maintain our own practices of self-denial than to perceive a fresh request from God for a sacrifice we are reluctant to make.

∼

Ordinarily, God is asking not for a heroism that will be admired by others, but for the self-effacement of an unnotable fidelity, a perseverance that draws no eyes. He asks of us a concealed heroism that never escapes for long a companionship with the fatigue of unrewarding efforts. This quiet steadiness is impossible without a spirit of greater interior mortification.

～

Without some exercises of mortification, a soul will continue to covet. This is a consequence of failing to temper tendencies toward pleasure for its own sake. The most immediate effect is a weaker quality of eye. Coveting is pernicious to our spiritual vision. It makes our eyes impure, narrowing them in desire, making them filter many observations of a day through a lens of inner need. Coveting is first in the eyes, eyes hungry for satisfaction, before they find anything to pursue. Without learning to deny ourselves, coveting will be last in our eyes as well, eyes overcome by frustration because we have not learned to seek blindly after God.

～

A certain disregard for self is a condition for advancing in a passion for God as the dominant desire of one's life. The extent to which we object to this statement as fanatical and extreme, or argue its unhealthy psychological implications, or simply dismiss it as a pious exaggeration, may reflect how little we have pondered the actual lives of saints.

~

In facing temptation there is no reliable defense other than prayer and our capacity for renunciation. Temptation can come at surprising times; it is unpredictable. Sometimes there is not enough calm to overcome it by a quick mental resistance. We must simply take grip of a desire for God, fighting the uncertainty of outcome, trusting in a rescue. The reprieve may come without our deeper notice. In the meantime it can seem a terrible wait. The truth is that if prayer is aroused a hidden intervention is immediate, like a mother rushing to the cry of her child. What may seem a lonely resistance conceals the hidden presence of God. Renunciation and prayer draw always the aid of God.

~

There can be days when we desire in prayer a more radical offering to God, and then, later, turn casually away from a small sacrifice because it does not seem significant enough for our aspiration. A deeper surrender to God is delayed in that refusal. What God asks of us is often found in the small hour, the small gesture, the small gift. It may be the most trivial mortifications we refuse that keep a greater awareness of his hidden presence from lighting up within our soul. God's concealed presence requires an alertness to these subtle promptings to sacrifice. If we do not deny ourselves in smaller ways, we may soon prefer a God who blesses our own biases and propensities. Unfortunately, this God is not real. God is close to us when we make ourselves accessible to his requests. This means to expect small testings in which our own preference has often to be denied. If we avoid this and find ways around it, the God who hides may be more concealed and unreachable when we do pray.

∼

A more intense passion for God discovered in prayer is bound to diminish our regard for the pleasures of this world. Without much effort we may find ourselves after prayer somewhat indifferent to worldly amusements. Sometimes this means a confused discomfort with innocuous enjoyments. It might seem a strange form of blessing, until we experience a strong desire for prayer just at an hour when an innocent diversion is felt as empty and banal. This realization may increase a desire to strip one's life more in poverty. In renouncing unnecessary comforts, a different motive begins to clarify. We are not engaged simply in a spiritual discipline of penance. Often without realizing it, we are disposing ourselves for a more personal encounter with God. The hope of every sacrifice of comfort can be that in deprivation and poverty we may come to know the God who embraces beggars and lepers with a divine kiss.

10

Suffering and Trial

"Someone wounds our soul with a wound which will never heal, and it is through that wound that He finds His way to the very center of our being."

—Augustín Guillerand

"All knowledge of God is but a kind of recognition. The true way of knowing God is to suffer oneself to be known by Him."

—Charles Journet

"If there is no limit to what God asks of us, it is because there is no limit to what he wishes to give us."

—Abbé Henri Huvelin

The experience of suffering can at times involve a loss of confidence in God's near presence. It is easy to imagine a divine neglect of the soul when suffering continues unabated. The hiddenness of God can intensify and cause greater anguish inasmuch as his seeming absence does not alter. The challenge of suffering is a test to all sanctity. It is met well whenever the truth of God's presence is embraced in a deeper certitude of faith. The certitude is directed precisely at the concealed truth of God's nearness whenever external evidence seems to contradict this truth.

The psychologists are sometimes quick to remind us that forcing any painful experience into a forgotten corner of the soul is likely to do eventual harm. But if we have ignored this warning, it is good to remember that God entered that corner as well, and that he is still waiting there with an offer of his friendship if our soul wishes to meet him. Some people may only realize the extent to which God has been secretly giving himself when they perceive that his companionship has all along been present in that hidden corner of the soul.

∽

It is a repeated observation of Saint John of the Cross that God prostrates souls in a preliminary trial when he intends to draw closer in love. Here a pattern is noted, calling for our insight. No doubt we need to understand the providence of God differently. Trials do not reflect a sign of disfavor with God. Rather, the reverse is indicated. God is offering an invitation, even if it hardly seems so. He is teaching, even if it seems a harsh lesson. It may be a hard truth to accept that God's greater love is proven by the prevalence of trials we could not foresee, and by their lingering despite every plea for their removal. It is a rare soul that learns to take no surprise at this. There are indeed many shocks in what can seem God's rough treatment. Perhaps it is not unusual that we attempt to persuade God to be more gentle in his manner. It appears sometimes that nothing moves him in this regard. More love for God, for example, rather than overcoming a trial, will seem on occasion to extend the duration of a time of trial. But at the end of the day we face always the same question. Would we prefer to love less if it meant not to suffer?

~

When we confront pain, trying to see as God sees is usually futile and presumptuous. Nonetheless God asks more than a mere grudging acceptance of his will in any suffering. It is true that God's refusal to explain himself in a time of trial often leaves us little option but a blind trust in his divine providence. But this should not encourage passive submission on our part. In fact, when our faith is blind, an act of profound surrender must accompany it, along with the awareness of a truth. This is that everything God permits is inseparable from a very personal love he extends to us in a trial. Faith takes a large step when it passes from a degree of respect for the divine prerogative in trials to a real wonder at the apparent fervor of divine love in this regard —a fervor we may sometimes wish would diminish a bit.

~

We have to be careful at times not to pray "thy will be done" as if a secret agreement is present by which no divine testing in our life can take place without our approval. The words, rich as they are, are empty without our willingness to embrace unwelcome advances by God asking our soul to offer more.

~

The idea that there are random acts by God from a kind of divine caprice, without plan or purpose, cannot be. It would be like thinking that God does not focus his attention properly. The notion is absurd and unacceptable. And yet it seems at times that we are subject to events which a little divine management might have prevented. It is easy then to imagine that we are outside God's interest, that he must be taken up with more important matters, leaving us to mishap and a turn of fate. But are not such thoughts equally unreal? Many times we must simply accept that we are small and incapable of perceiving God's hidden ways, no more than a child can understand what it is to think the thoughts of an adult.

～

Among followers of a crucified Lord are sharp divergences regarding the prospect of suffering. At one extreme can be a worrisome fear that God plans to test the soul eventually in some grave manner. The anxious thought is that the clock ticks toward an hour of hardship which allows no preparation other than knowledge of its inevitability. Suffering even of a lesser magnitude disturbs a soul fearful in this way. Another tendency has variations. It is to regard trials as likely, as recurring and repeatable, yet not to be feared. A response has already proved calming in previous difficulties —that God is present in every difficulty, that every trial invites an offering to God. The finer approach, however, is to perceive in the inevitability of suffering a mark of divine love. It is to welcome the prospect of further offerings as means of union with a beloved who hung on a cross. The thought of suffering does not frighten. It has been understood in love.

～

Some spiritual writing of old advocated a spirit of resignation to God's will in time of trial. This meant a docility toward the will of God, an acceptance of events determined by the hand of God. But the word resignation is easily misinterpreted. A passivity can enter the notion and distort it. We may neglect to offer ourselves with vigor to God's choice, instead simply bearing up, refraining from resistance, adopting an air of defeat without a fight. Suffering requires instead a very active faith. But this is not simply in order to endure. We must see suffering in a graced light. Our true powerlessness rises up in the face of suffering. Indeed an incomprehension often accompanies suffering. God's purpose is unknown; he is more hidden. Precisely then must faith be exercised. God is inviting us to himself long before our last breath, and we must come to realize this. Our profound surrender to him is his desire, so different from mere resignation to his will. This deeper surrender is what God waits for always; it is why he allows pain.

~

A stoic blunting of sensibility can provide a barrier against pain, but this is costly in a spiritual sense. And one of the more subtle costs is that in feeling less, we may imagine we have a sign that we are giving ourselves more fully to God's will—the sign being that God has rewarded us with an indifference toward suffering.

~

We are likely to show more of our soul to others in our time of suffering—more than we realize. A transparency usually accompanies human trial and need. There is less behind which to hide. However, it may only be that a poverty always present in our soul is no longer so unknown and secret. Of course it is never hidden from the eyes of God. But we can forget that when all seems comfortable and secure.

~

Resentment at suffering—gall and curses and spleen —the denial of meaning in suffering: all this may have in it a trepidation about God. There are people who believe that God uses suffering to punish in this life. And many who embrace this thought are convinced they deserve suffering even as they resent the sign they think it manifests of divine displeasure. They cannot separate suffering from a visceral pessimism about God in their own regard. At the very least this is a reason to refrain from too facile a commentary on God's love in a time of suffering. For it is precisely a love that is shrouded and concealed that confuses these souls.

~

Suffering has, concealed within it, a longing for God. There is a desire that God show himself, and perhaps a strong confidence that he will intervene soon. On the other hand, mild forms of despair can accompany longer trials. Somehow, without realizing how it fades, the expectation of a rescue from God disappears, replaced by a fear that God's intervention, once considered only a matter of time, is no longer forthcoming. Suffering that goes on without respite can bring, as well, a sense of God's absence or of his reproach. Then the longing is for some reassurance from God. We can easily get lost in narrow corridors of anxious questioning, finding a cause for trial in our own offensiveness to God. This mood of unworthiness may continue unless we choose to believe that God places us in trial only to expose his love for us. At certain times when God hides, faith requires a quite stubborn exercise. We may not feel God's presence. But our faith must embrace a certainty that God remains constant in his presence despite every outward turbulence sweeping over us.

~

Having spiritual courage cannot mean overpowering trials. It means accepting that some trials do not pass lightly but rather take up a permanent residence in our lives and age along with us. The courage then is not in determining to put up a tough-minded fight. It is in conceding to divine providence the sovereign right to return in various guises of discomfort to draw our deeper submission to the divine will.

⁓

Sudden epiphanies of the divine purpose in trials are not likely. The opposite is more common. Indeed a question why God has allowed a trial may not release us until its unanswerability is at last accepted. Sometimes the suffering of this is longer when a passion to know why God has chosen some suffering for us is inflamed by our own lack of humility. On the other hand, a prayer of gratitude to God precisely for what is costly and difficult to understand often has an uncanny spiritual effect. Admittedly, such a prayer is difficult. But the expression of thanks for what is not yet understood has a mysterious way of allowing God to remain close in a time of difficulty. Perhaps this occurs because such a prayer is impossible without humility.

⁓

How is it that sometimes we glimpse hidden suffering in another person even in our first contact? Why more quickly in some instances than in

others? Is it only because a person in this case is un-
guarded, perhaps unaware of the inner distress
shown visibly in that moment? Or is it rather a
shared quality of soul that provokes the likelihood
of this recognition? What then does this say of our
own soul when we perceive an effort in another
person to conceal some private suffering?

∼

"It is finished" (Jn 19:30). We would like to make
these sacred words of Jesus our own when a spiritual trial shows no sign of easing. But it may be the
nature of every deeper trial of soul that it concludes
only when we are emptied entirely. And when does
that occur? Spiritual trials, even when they seem
to fade away, adopt different disguises. They trade
places and replace each other. All the while an on-
going purification of soul is taking place. This purification approaches its end only when what is taken
from us exceeds everything we would surrender on
our own to God. It will cease when we have nothing to give of our own, when perhaps God may
seize from us even the poverty and emptiness we
have begun to savor.

∼

Can we suffer trials of any kind and be content at
the same time? Only perhaps when our prayer ac-

cepts an absence of explanation from God. Otherwise a trial that does not pass can bring restless thoughts, upsetting and agitating our soul. If we do not find a certain quiet of mind in our prayer at such times, questions about God are almost inevitable. They whisper that God is inconsiderate in his distribution of trials, that he listens only to favored souls, that he is weary of us. The only sound option is to let go of a need for understanding God. This is not to endure stupidly, adopting a mindless state. It is to cast our soul into the dust and noise of Calvary, leaving the meaning of a painful time to a later recognition.

~

It is unfortunate if after many signs of solicitude on God's part we allow ourselves to be intimidated by the hypothetical thought of trials yet to come. Admittedly, we can tire of divine testings. We can put God on notice that we have had enough. But perhaps we would forfeit a great attraction for God that was growing in our soul. We forget that he may find us more appealing in our poor trials than at any other hour.

I I

The Poor

"When you are weary of praying, and do not receive, consider how often you have heard a poor man calling, and have not listened to him."

—Saint John Chrysostom

"After the resurrection . . . Jesus no longer wanted to be touched except through his wounds."

—Blaise Pascal

"Beware the Jesus who passes by and does not return."

—Jacques Maritain

The concealment of God is a quite literal truth in Jesus' presence in the poor. Beneath the scars and disfigurement of poverty is hidden an exalted truth—the incarnate Son's promise of his own real presence in the life of the poor man. The contemplative is always the first to embrace this truth. It is a privilege, in a sense, of the contemplative pursuit of a God who hides and disguises himself. Once again an irony presents itself. The greatness of the contemplative life is not confined to cloisters and monasteries. It thrives as well in those places where the presence of Jesus hides in the poorest of the poor.

"What you do to the least of my brothers, you do to me" (Mt 25:40). It is the nature of a mystical truth of this sort that its significance is easily missed when first heard. That is why it is often neglected even in charities to the poor. The reason is understandable. The appearance of real poverty is unmajestic, dirty, sometimes revolting. Nothing divine suggests itself. Only a kind of mystical realism pierces the shocking truth that divinity hides beneath the offensive demeanor of a poor man. This truth assumes faith, great faith. Jesus' words in Matthew 25 move us only when understood quite literally in their meaning. Then it is realized that his promise has been kept. He invites us to touch his presence personally in the poor, to clasp the wounds of his crucifixion in the bodies of the poor.

∼

The poor are the last to suspect it. They grow accustomed to their want and isolation, their unworthy difference from others. They do not see in themselves what long dereliction and neglect have carved into their silent hours. For God it is better that way. They can assume their disguise secretly, in a concealment unknown to them. It is in this secrecy that our own testing and probing take place. For a poor man's eyes are never exclusively his own. Their lonely hunger hides another real presence, a mysterious vulnerability, waiting again to receive our gift or our refusal.

~

If God's way of hiding is to extend a beggar's hand toward us, it is remarkable that he allows himself to be refused without any reprisal. This is a mystery of humility not easily reconciled with the idea of God's omnipotence. In truth he becomes powerless before our whims and moods. Nonetheless it is not so surprising. Already in his life on earth Our Lord showed himself powerful in love by preferring lowliness. The abjection he now chooses is to become one with the poorest of the poor. It is indeed a real omnipotence once again that God manifests by becoming secretly united with the poor. Only a God who became man has the omnipotent power to offer his presence in this manner. For those who love him in the poor, his power to draw love in an appearance of powerless need is real and increasingly affecting.

~

Kalighat, Calcutta. Mother Teresa's Home for Dying Destitutes. The large room is lined with parallel tiers of closely positioned beds filled with poor men. Many are wasted and emaciated, all bones, dying from lung diseases after years as manual rickshaw drivers breathing close at hand the gas fumes of the congested Calcutta streets. In the midst of activity among the patients by the sisters and volunteers, one sister passes slowly from bed to bed. She moves along the top tier, then across and down the line, speaking a few words, grasping a hand, brushing a forehead, sitting on some beds. She finishes and leaves the room. At the end her face looks weary, no longer smiling, as though she had been searching for someone she thought was hiding in that room and did not find.

∼

The amazing thing is that Jesus spoke the words of Matthew 25 only on the brink of his Passion. As the gospel narrative continues into the next chapter, we are told that "after saying these things Jesus said, 'You know that *after two days* the passover is coming and the Son of Man will be handed over to be crucified.' " The phrase "after two days" means very likely that the words of Matthew 25 were spoken on Holy Thursday at some time during the day. We know that the same words "after three days" in reference to the Resurrection will include the day of his death as the first day of the three. So, too, here. The astonishing link of Matthew 25 to the Passion occurs at the end of the crucifixion when Jesus pronounces his words, "I thirst" (Jn 19:28). He had earlier referred in Matthew 25 to the poor man thirsting who was either refused or given something to drink. Surely Jesus wanted the connection understood and pondered. It is a reason why he waited to deliver his address in Matthew 25 until this late hour. Indeed it is possible that a divine act occurred in Jesus' "I thirst", spoken just before his dying on the cross. With this pronouncement he unites himself with all human misery throughout history. The identification of Jesus with the poor man of all ages becomes a truth carved into every encounter we have with suffering. The poor man's thirst, in all its variations, is a perpetual reenactment of Jesus pronouncing again his thirst from the cross. Love or vinegar—these remain options until the end of time.

∼

The likelihood of these words from Matthew 25 being spoken on Holy Thursday links them as well to the sacramental concealment of Jesus' real presence in the Eucharist. In both cases a disguise in appearance hides the divine reality. They are of course not equivalent. The complete change of bread and wine into Christ's Body and Blood in transubstantiation is not the same as Jesus mysteriously uniting himself to a poor man. Nonetheless, in both cases we confront a mystery hidden within an appearance that defies the truth. In both cases our intensity of faith deepens our love for the real, personal presence of Jesus offering himself to our love. It should be no surprise that those who love prayer before the Eucharist are often drawn to the poor. Time spent with poor people is sometimes the door as well to being drawn to quiet time praying with the Eucharist. The concealment of God provokes the soul in both these mysteries.

∼

If the words in Matthew 25 mean what they say, what are the implications? Can Jesus use the gesture or words of a poor person to manifest himself in a mysterious manner? The possibility is real. A Missionary of Charity sister, for example, described herself sitting on the edge of a bed with a man who was only days from dying, trying that late morning to feed him some liquid gruel. While she was bringing the spoon to his lips, he gripped the religious garb of her sari tightly in his hand. The noon bell began to ring, requiring her to return to the convent. She asked him to release his hand from her sari, but he stared blankly and gave no response. She repeated her request and tried to pull his hand away. Finally she took from her belt a large metal crucifix, which she carried as part of her religious dress. She asked him to hold the cross in his hand. Immediately he let go of the sari and took the crucifix in his hand. Then she returned to the convent, but fretful now and anxious about losing her crucifix. Would it be there when she came back in the afternoon? She regretted giving away her cross. The thought troubled her that for some time she had been refusing sacrifices and a deeper spirit of offering. In the chapel her prayer became a plea to Jesus to recover her crucifix as a sign he accepted her new resolve. She would not refuse or forsake the cross again. No burden would be too great. Returning to the man's bed in the afternoon, she anticipated a struggle to pry his fingers from her crucifix. But when she leaned forward and requested her cross, at once the man gave it back with a strangely beautiful smile, as though he was not alone in his gesture.

～

Those like the sisters of Mother Teresa who touch closely the sufferings of the poor comment at times

how little a bodily sense aversion intrudes when a
real hunger for God accompanies this work. Nox-
ious smells, disfigurement, the horrors of disease
do not get in the way. They do not repel and in-
timidate in an aggressive manner. Instead a kind
of rapt attention can be turned toward the misery
of another human being. A deeper layer of soul
takes up the task of washing filth, dressing infested
wounds, or feeding a mad, twisted face. This is
clearly a blessing, not a momentary reprieve, that
natural repugnance disappears and the senses perceive differently. But perhaps it becomes for some
souls a lasting grace of self-forgetfulness, leaving
God free on certain days to hover with his presence strangely near and watching.

∼

There can be something akin to the intuitions of a
painter facing a scene of beauty in the response that
rises up spontaneously in a soul of great charity to
the poor. A readiness for discovery is operative in
both instances. Both the artist and one who loves
the poor have eyes that see more. A light is cast
upon observations, surprising with disclosures that
would otherwise be missed. Such persons respond
to clues, hints, small details that can otherwise pass
unnoticed. Just as sunlight unites with the eyes of

an artist when a striking scene provokes a desire to paint it, so, too, can God become a companion to the eyes. For a person who loves the poor, an encounter with distress or pain beneath outward features can draw the soul to the immediacy of a stark beauty exposed in the misery of a particular face.

～

We can never know with the poor whether the faces we observe are going to pass away, leaving no trace in our memory, or, very differently, whether the weariness and pain in a certain face will return to our mind and become our own at an hour when we thought ourselves to be content without companionship. This, too, may be a sign of Jesus' presence in that earlier encounter.

～

There is both knowledge of God and a great ignorance in most actions done to the poor. A poor man who attracts us more by asking nothing of us even as we are about to make an unexpected gift and shock him—is God's love for us like this when we are a bit obtuse and have no realization of his immense desire to give himself to us?

~

In a garbage-dump slum of Port-au-Prince, I was visiting the compound of the Brothers' branch of the Missionaries of Charity. Accompanied by an Italian brother of the congregation, we passed through many rooms of bedridden men in the patients' section. As the brother crossed the doorway into the last room, a bright smile in a dark face greeted him from the bed immediately facing the door. A young man about twenty was very pleased to see this brother. The brother approached the bed and said he had medical work to do for him. He readied gauze, scissors, and ointment before pulling back the sheet. The young man had lost his leg, amputated at the thigh—the result of a truck striking him in a crowded street. The brother took much care slowly changing the bandages. All the while the young man, now in much pain, was brushing his hand lightly over the forearm of the brother, not interfering, never pulling the arm away, simply repeating this calm, gentle contact. The whole time he stared intently at the face of the brother, as though awaiting a return glance. The stare of those eyes seemed to contain a plea for recognition that now, in my memory, is more than human. Likewise the gesture of brushing the brother's arm now seems also beyond a merely human action. A year later I visited again and learned that the brother had departed the congregation. Is it possible that Jesus was offering a sign of reassurance to this religious brother in the mysterious intensity of that poor man's look and gesture?

More intense love is not an impulse to impracticality. But anyone living under its sway will sometimes live imprudently, even recklessly, with no concern for tomorrow. Intense love sweeps away reserve and caution, as the gospel shows in the old widow casting her last coins away. There is no thought then for correctness or consequence. Such actions may be misunderstood or draw murmurs, missed for a beauty buried in the outward features of a negligible gesture. But great acts of love, as this one, often take place in this manner. Perhaps they are most quickly learned in actions of love to the poor: learned there because it is the mysterious attraction of Jesus in the poor man that compels these extravagant generosities.

Anyone working closely with the poor comes to realize in a certain sense the practical futility of what is being done. A desire for lasting achievement cannot sustain this work. The poor assisted are the poor who do not disappear. It takes a disinterested and pure love, looking toward nothing beyond the immediacy of actions, to keep a person persevering in service to the poor one singular day after another. But this means above all that the concealed image of Jesus Christ is sought stubbornly, lovingly in this time with the poor.

⁓

Practical efforts on behalf of the poor, while noble in themselves, can also be oblivious to the truth of Matthew 25. A literal meaning of these words demands a recognition: every appearance of misery conceals the face of God. When Our Lord promised that the poor would remain with us always, he pledged his enduring presence in our midst. The poor are never simply the poor. They are the poor who hide Jesus himself. Without an awareness of the promise in Matthew 25, every endeavor to provide material benefits for the poor can also be a way of ignoring God. The disturbing appearance of poverty that hides God among us requires more than zeal simply to remove it.

⁓

There is no way to foresee what will trigger it, what odd gesture of poverty will ignite a burning sympathy for someone who was not so loved an hour before. The emotion felt is out of proportion with the glance that precipitates it. The man I was visiting in the hospital was propped up with pillows and lying on his back in the bed. His hands were folded and resting on his chest. The blue veins in his bony hands stood out. His eyes were shut; I thought he might be praying. Lightly I called his name and the sound startled him awake. Then the hands with the fingers still entwined tried to rise up. But they were stuck together, caught and helpless for the moment. Suspended in the air, they began to tremble until they pulled apart with a soundless snap. One hand found the sheet and lifted it as though a board of wood blanketed him. They crawled beneath like scared children fleeing some danger. I remembered how he used to shake hands when he was healthy and strong, a hard grip that refused to be overmatched. Now he was shriveled to skin and bones in the last weeks of a slow cancer. And his eyes looked frightened that I had come expecting from him the same handshake.

~

Among the homeless poor whose lives mingle with the litter of the streets, a nuisance to many in their grime and smell and soliciting eye, not all are deranged and lunatic. Surely some are true souls of despair who have embraced a life of forsakenness to enclose and silence within themselves a mistake now long past. And if these latter have a stifled passion we do not suspect, and a recurring thought that another life was possible with a different choice, in some cases the occupied faces hurrying past them may share more kinship than they realize with their own crossroad, when they could have chosen differently.

⌢

"The poor you have always with you" (Jn 12:8). And yet it is rather easy to look at the derelict poor and consider self-inflicted the scars from alcohol and drugs that mar their faces—easy to harbor disdain for their indecency. But then surely we sometimes miss a lonely man's eyes looking up in a wish that his face will not provoke this time a glance of revulsion. And perhaps the same look of these eyes was also in the eyes of Jesus as he carried the cross to Calvary.

⌢

The desire to love a poor man at first contact with his suffering is already an encounter with the Son of God who took our flesh. The desire we feel to love a poor man is indeed a sacred request from God himself. But we have to have courage to believe he is speaking to us in that desire. The easier option is to ignore the thought that Jesus is drawing us when a poor man evokes our sympathy. Yet that thought sometimes does not disappear. It lingers and disturbs. How can we keep walking if Jesus is hiding himself in this poor man's misery? But we need spiritual courage to elevate our faith to this sacred truth.

～

Is it surprising that souls who devote their lives to the poor are drawn to the beauty of a "hidden life"? The constant return to the concealed presence of Jesus Christ in the poor inclines them to embrace a love for their own concealment. These are people who search for secret acts of charity unseen by others. They have grown accustomed to the divine preference for secret encounters with their own soul in the disguises of the poor. Their experience of a real presence of God in the poor inclines them in turn to esteem highly a hidden gift of their soul to God. And they express this quite concretely in a thousand small ways in daily works with the poor.

～

The hidden presence of Jesus in the poor invokes a need to conceal ourselves also from our own eyes. This is a necessity for greater love: to disappear inside our actions, unconcerned for self. More intense love in actions demands this spirit of hiddenness. We have an impetus to hiddenness in every encounter with the poor. The concealment of Our Lord in the poor draws a desire to forget ourselves when we are with the poor. It is a mysterious gift that accompanies being with the poor. We lose thought of self with the poor because the suffering of the poor overcomes thought of self. It is Our Lord, actually, who is drawing us away from self.

12

Contemplatives

"God often isolates those whom He chooses, so that we have nowhere to turn except to Him, and then He reveals Himself to us."

—Seraphim Rose

"Men of prayer are the happiest and also the unhappiest of men."
—John Ruysbroeck

"We must remember that the best way of hiding anything is to make it common, to place it among the most ordinary objects."

—Jacques Maritain

The contemplative is a hidden soul, disguised and yet also transparent. The concealment of God finds its way into the deeper spiritual impulses of contemplative souls. Their union with God draws them to a preference for remaining unknown except to the eyes of God in heaven. At the same time contemplatives display notable qualities besides their penchant for a hidden quality. These point to their intense drive to give themselves to God in an exclusive manner. Their interior lives overflow inevitably into their visible lives—just as God's hidden life expresses itself in visible manifestations of his infinite love.

When God wants a life for himself in an uncommon way, he provokes a love for the secrecy of the offer he is making. A contemplative impulse to a kind of spiritual privacy often results, a desire to remain unknown to all except God. The practical consequence is to disappear in some form of hiddenness with God. This inclination is not without spiritual logic. Intense love for a God who conceals himself provokes a longing for a life obscurely alone with him. These are souls that happily embrace hardship, renunciation, anonymity in monasteries, cloisters, or the congregations that take their lives to the poorest corners of the world. They have in common that God hides within their lives and they seek to find that place of hiding by disappearing themselves from the eyes of men.

∽

Despite all that is recounted of them, the great truth of the saints was hidden from public view, a truth layered within clefts and crevices, a secret ultimately incommunicable and never fully uncovered. The essential truth of who they were remained enclosed in the silence of their private exchanges with God. Every saint was a contemplative, in other words, carrying on a secret, intensifying exchange of self-giving with God. We never see the fullness of this from the outside.

~

In their caves or cloisters or on noisy city streets, the contemplatives are a hiding place for God. He hollows out in them a secret refuge for his presence. By God's designs they may often go through life unnoticed except by souls searching for God. It is indeed one of the finer triumphs of religious truth —the fervent desire for God in certain lives that may be largely unobserved, a great passion of soul hiding behind ordinariness. Some souls attract primarily the attention of God, and he prefers apparently to keep it that way. Their lack of distinction in anything the world values, their unadaptability to worldliness, is essential to the gift God bestows on them and the use he makes of them. While passing at times inconspicuously through life, these souls nonetheless leave their mark on others, mysteriously, undeniably. They are a sign of the great fecundity of love a human heart can possess when it becomes poor. And they confirm God's penchant for disguising himself in insignificance, a truth as constant as the presence of Christ concealed in the Eucharist.

~

What is being expressed by the word holy? Perhaps it is a comment on the observable features of a person, such as a profusion of generous actions and a joy in them. But we cannot see the more intense truth which resides within holiness, its contemplative quality. It may be, for instance, that all holiness, like all contemplative life, entails a dissatisfaction of soul, only at times relieved. It apparently drives certain lives in a need to give always more to God, which they cannot ignore without causing pain to themselves. It cannot be an unhappy state they are in. Yet at the same time these souls are dissatisfied, always reaching out toward more. It means also that they are not so peaceful as we first think from their exterior appearance.

~

The spirituality of contemplatives is linked always to purifications. These souls are shaped and branded by purifications. Their passion for God is inseparable from a persevering love they exercise throughout the pruning God exacts upon them. Perhaps this spiritual intensity eventually touches everything in their relations with God—not only their acts of love, but their struggles and trials and frustrations in love. Once a passion for God reaches a certain point, refusing him even something small seems to inflict anguish upon these souls. This, too,

the contemplatives suffer more acutely, but only because they have a passion for God that makes them
already very poor. The intensity of their discontent
corresponds to the love possessing their souls.

~

Three things experienced by Jesus Christ on the
cross are likely to occur to some degree in the life
of the contemplative. Jesus became poor—stripped
of every possession, of His dignity, of any respect
from the world. He was forsaken spiritually—lost,
in darkness internally, without consoling awareness. He was afflicted by thirst—unrelieved, with
no one, nothing, to diminish his suffering. Such a
self-stripping passion, even if it must be much less
intense than that of Jesus, is a possibility a contemplative sooner or later must accept.

~

Something akin to a kind of spiritual violence can
seem to mark divine actions toward a soul close to
God, a contemplative soul. Perhaps we do not ac-
knowledge it so easily for fear of inviting the same
into our lives. The violent dimension is eminently
spiritual, yet it often enough involves a person in a
loss of health or another trial of some lasting magnitude. In all its variations this violence will involve

some crushing of the soul with an awareness of its own insignificance. In this suffering the soul will come to realize an impotence in itself, an incapacity to free itself on its own. Often no reversal of fortune takes place, no rescue from events. Rather, all in a life joins to reinforce a steady reduction of the soul to its nothingness before God. This is the violence of love at work, drawing a soul toward an absolute surrender to divine love.

～

In some contemplative souls it seems that love for God becomes like a thorn impossible to dislodge from the heart. These souls suffer from love as from a wound. In one sense love is for them an irritant, a constant vexing presence, even as they have no inclination to assuage or remove it. It makes them at times unhappy in love, if that is possible. These are souls who are humbled by the deprivations they experience interiorly, but in a manner that has no resentment, no complaint. In some cases they are souls who little realize, during their lives, how close they are to God.

～

There is no contemplative life without the poverty of an exterior self permeating awareness in a more painful manner over time. This may be why some contemplative souls never overcome a strain of discomfort in company with people they are not close to. There is a reason, it seems. Their hours of silence stripped of human contact open them to their own poverty. The poverty of solitude makes them vulnerable in a certain way, leaving them exposed and naked when they venture into social gatherings. At such times the exterior self can seem a flimsy veneer of unimportance, insubstantial and contrived. Some of them give the impression they would prefer to remain exclusively under the gaze of God's eyes, where alone they are at ease. There is a certain regular pattern in this. Contemplative souls, wherever they live, are often to some extent humiliated souls—but only because God draws closer to their poverty in this manner.

$\sim$

Where to find souls of deeper interiority, contemplative souls? Among the crowds and coteries vying for recognition from one another, seeking attention for themselves? A true interior soul is found only when these drives are conquered. These souls are of course not just in cloisters and monasteries, living in solitude. Some may be living next to us. There is no unmistakable sign to indicate them, but if we look closer we may notice a hint. Even while content or affable or engaging, they are captive to a solitude they cannot escape even in company with others. But of course they are not actually alone. They have a companionship even when it may seem they are plunged far into their desert aloneness.

~

A contemplative life signifies in one sense an emptiness of desire toward all that is not God. This does not mean an indifference to everything else in life. It does mean, though, a fading of interest in self. The contemplatives, it seems, lose a desire for pleasing self. This must be a fruit of their prayer. After a time they want only what God wants to give, nothing more, even when this means deprivation in prayer. They come to trust a deeper concealed truth of his presence that is beyond any experience of their own poverty. The desert experienced in their soul is accepted as a fitting condition for the vast expanses of God's love.

~

Contemplatives seem to possess often a perspicuity of the eyes. Their eyes are quick and intuitive in grasping truth in what they see in other souls, in cutting to essentials. This perceptiveness is surely from their prayer. They have long turned their inner desire in prayer toward God, to a truth beyond self. And this disposition carries over into encounters outside prayer. Their attention is a turn of love toward the other. The result is a more intense receptivity outside prayer to what is present before their eyes. They see more because they love more. There may be another reason as well for their eyes seeing more. Contemplatives have much experience of waiting in prayer, and of delay. This carries over outside prayer. They bring a patience with them outside prayer, and it brings a perspicuity to their human encounters: the poverty that ordinarily hides within souls opens to view before their eyes with little resistance. It can be uncanny, in fact, how quickly contemplatives sometimes penetrate to the inner truth of souls. In their presence it may seem as though our own poverty has been waiting all along for a recognition from such eyes.

$\sim$

In contemplative souls, there is sometimes a reluctance to speak of God. Perhaps it is at first a contradiction that makes no sense. They shy away from talking of personal relations with God. Their lives give witness certainly that God is everything to them. But at the same time there is this silence. They seem to have no words to articulate what we desire to hear. If they do speak of God, they reveal more by a tone of voice, or by a silence in the midst of sentences, the great longing for God that is in their soul. Their passion reaches up out of their silence into their few spoken words. We may wish they would speak of God, but their lives and the silence itself have become a superior form of communication. They are souls of prayer and theirs is a different way of speaking of God.

∼

The first words addressed by Jesus to Andrew and presumably to John—"what are you looking for?" —hide in every contemplative's encounter with God (Jn 1:38). This question is the subdued provocation in prayer always waiting to be heard. The contemplative listens to it as John did, allowing this question to remain in the soul for a lifetime, refraining from any conclusive reply. It cannot be answered by the external circumstances of a life. The answer God seeks is discovered only in silence and love. That same silence covers over any response, never permitting this question to be neglected for any longer time. It is answered without words by the yearning and thirst of the soul for God.

~

"I will lead the blind on their journey; by paths unknown I will guide them" (Is 42:16). We must be willing to remain in the discomfort of blindness if we are to be led properly into contemplative graces. If we insist on peering ahead, calculating the steps to be taken, determining the goal that must be pursued, we forsake the unseen hand of guidance that is taking us toward a goal beyond our expectation. Without an acceptance of blindness, soon enough we try to shake free and enter a false spiritual path, seeking out a chimera of our own making. We lose the way that leads to a contemplative union with God. This is true of both our interior life of prayer and our service to others in work and activity.

~

It may be in contemplative lives that a crossroad arrives one day to sacrifice every right of determination over the future, to renounce definitively the impulse to forecast or predict. The soul simply offers its remaining days to God, leaving what is to come to God's choice. Surrender to God in any full sense perhaps demands this sacrifice. It allows God to lead as he sees fit, without our consultation or advice. At the same time this surrender is never concluded. After a certain interlude it must again be made in prayer.

~

One common sign of contemplative holiness is a greater spiritual passion for intercession. The needs of others dominate attention more in these souls. This cannot be deflected; it becomes irrefusable. Contemplative souls seem to carry the solicitation of others without strain, almost effortlessly. There is no inclination to escape and hide from the request for prayer. The appeal of the other strikes home, reaching deeper regions of the soul, where love welcomes the entry of all who come as a stranger in need. The readiness to intercede is a sign of what may be a permanent disposition in heaven. The saints in heaven are souls who intercede without rest, and it may be they do this in a manner much like the request of Mary the contemplative to Jesus regarding her brother Lazarus —"the one whom you love is ill" (Jn 11:3). For surely it was the contemplative soul who composed the simple and bare words of this request.

~

The contemplative is not afraid to be a servant, which is a courage more necessary than it is thought at first. As part of the calling, the ideal servants in the world must live with a quality of concealment. It is a discipline of the servant's profession: their taste is unsolicited, their advice unsought. A self-renunciation must accompany their availability to the requests of another. If they begrudge their silence, they forfeit an indispensable condition of their service—an indifference to their own preference. What, then, does it mean to be a true servant of God in any setting but to live an analogous form of sacrifice? If necessary, a servant of God must happily embrace real insignificance, casting the self away and replacing it with a pure longing to serve in love.

∼

"I have seen that all perfection has an end; but your commands are boundless" (Ps 119:96). A clear tension is implicit in these words—a true contemplative challenge. There is a limited capacity within the soul for love; we can never love to infinitude. And yet God seems never to rest long in provoking within a soul the need to go further in love. The demands of love are indeed boundless and never diminish in intensity as long as a soul continues to offer itself to divine love.

13

Last Thoughts

"Faith and love are like the blind man's guides. They will lead you along a path unknown to you, to the place where God is hidden."

—Saint John of the Cross

"Only the silent hear and those who do not remain silent do not hear."
—Josef Pieper

"This world is, and always will be, a place of exile and pilgrimage; a desert to be crossed, where for a moment we pitch our tent, soon to strike it again and continue our journey."

—Augustín Guillerand

The aphorism and short reflection can be a stimulant to contemplative insights. The brief thought may hide implications to be uncovered and pondered. Short statements invite us to linger and ruminate for a moment, resisting the impulse to seek only knowledge and nothing more. They remind us of a need to wait for God when we pray in silence, not moving on too quickly. The quiet interlude, the silent pause, can be a setting for God to speak. A spirit of receptivity to God in that silence can be a catalyst to grace. Perhaps God hides himself in these silent interludes, waiting to be heard.

If divine favors are received at times in prayer, it is never because diligent efforts earn them or a correct manner of praying has been discovered. Much more, it is the poverty we experience in every greater striving for God which attracts favor from God. But this is usually understood as a form of blessing only after not comprehending.

∿

It is a simple truth of prayer that our soul will pass more lightly, more freely, more securely into the hiding places of God when we do not seek to overcome our blindness in silent prayer.

∿

It is surely a law of spiritual life that we will have only superficial access to real intimacy with God as long as we do not relinquish a quest for passing "experiences" of God.

∿

No spiritual purification, indeed, no particular testing from God can be anticipated except in the most generic fashion, like the knowledge of a foreign country that comes from perusing a picture book.

～

There is no such thing as a successful foray into seeking God in silent prayer; no one returns home with a prize in hand.

～

One of the necessary tasks of prayer is to persevere in an interior offering to Our Lord in the silence of prayer, even if the meager results of our scattered efforts outside prayer incline us to a periodic discouragement.

～

Concealment may be the manner by which God remains close to every soul he favors. But there is unlikely to be any soul, however saintly, who learns to find this entirely to its taste.

～

Jesus Christ as a man and as our God must be a constant desire in our prayer, never permitted to disappear from our soul's longing even in a deeper experience of our ignorance toward the mystery of God.

~

The voice of Jesus that speaks in the gospel pages is the same voice that hides in the language of divine silence. But if we do not hear the one, we are unlikely to hear the other.

~

It is a certain stubbornness of soul in continuing to offer ourselves to God in prayer, even when our external actions do not display an equivalent love, that may prepare in us a recognition of our powerlessness to love except as a gift from God.

~

Over time we ought to discover that a single need returns in prayer which has little to do with the various reflections we undertake: namely, a longing for God beneath our thought, at the core of our being.

~

"Lately in prayer", in the words of a contemplative, "I have been roaming around in a search I did not realize would frustrate my soul, seeking to enjoy God's presence close at hand, when he was waiting as usual for the simple offering of my love in the current hour.''

~

Perhaps we pray better when our soul finds very poor the words we have just used, words quickly surpassed by a deeper longing of soul that accompanies the return of silence to our prayer.

~

The gratuity of every grace of purification in prayer is matched by its precariousness. All advancement in prayer is at risk if we mistake purification for a problem to be solved, instead of an expression of God's love to be embraced.

~

Once we are fully committed to prayer, we should be ready for many days of silent, solitary prayer in which Our Lord seems to allow us only a gaze toward a receding horizon slowly descending into nightfall.

~

Interpreting an experience of painful aloneness in the interior life may depend on answering a question that God at some point may address to every soul searching earnestly for him—"Who, my child, is hiding from whom?"

～

We should ask the contemplatives in certain cases whether something close to an inner despair about themselves led in time to their more profound discovery of God's personal love and predilection.

～

In some lives, loving God may entail over time a shipwrecked manner of loving—cold and tired and holding on, clinging to broken wood, swept along currents they cannot master, yet knowing always that they cannot drown.

～

Only after purifications have been endured for a sufficient period of time do we realize that the dust and ashes tasted on some days in silent prayer are the remnant of a former self that has been slowly burning away in divine fire.

～

There are souls who allow prayer to fade from their lives because they interpret difficulty in prayer as a sign of their own indisposition for it. It is an easy step from an experience of distaste with prayer to the thought of its apparent irrelevance. Concluding an absence of any pragmatic value in prayer can be swift.

～

Distractions in prayer, while often uncontrollable, can be a type of forgetfulness. It is possible to become unwittingly rude and aloof with God, as though someone were in the same room with us and yet overlooked, our eyes preferring a scene of play outside the window.

～

The cost for certain forms of peace of mind is the loss of a passion for God. It is much better in prayer, at least for a time, to be restless or agitated in our search for God than to find tranquillity in a manner that leaves God safely distant and unable to disturb us.

～

A chase after spirituality is not the same as a genuine search for God. The former is likely to be accompanied by imaginative skills and illusions about self, and obstruct a more sober recognition that God must be sought in what may seem the uneventful tedium of a sacrificing life.

~

If our prayer does not regularly conclude in gratitude, something is lacking in our humility before God. The very nature of prayer, even in its struggle and occasional frustration, is to convey awareness of an immense, undeserved privilege.

~

A regrettable loss of prayer sometimes has its beginnings in the effort not to appear to others as a person caught up in excessive religious interest. And sometimes this is a temptation just at a time when the life of prayer is becoming a greater attraction.

~

Sometimes priests who advance in an ecclesial career are disinclined to the practice of private prayer. The lack of taste for prayer done quietly and alone, with none but God's eyes in attendance, apparently strikes no dissonance with a stronger desire felt for serving the Church in noticeably public ways.

～

Spiritually, it can be propitious that we experience some loneliness after a time of easy companionship with others. We may find in prayer a more intense longing for God which we had allowed to fade when friendships were close at hand.

～

Intellectually, we may affirm that divine providence is at work in our lives. But what does this mystery mean if not an immense desire on God's part to stretch a secret hand of companionship across eternity into the present day with a divine longing that we might, like a beggar, grasp it in surprised joy?

～

The most exalted truths of faith cannot be separated from mundane spiritual implications. These doctrinal truths, most especially of God taking our flesh, reach into the smallest choices of a day, where the poor man of Nazareth hides again in disguise.

～

A person's vision will always change if the soul grows in a contemplative passion for God. An intense longing for God lingers in the eyes after leaving prayer, making them more searching, more dissatisfied, more blind and groping, perhaps without knowing what it is they aspire to see.

~

It can be expected that a God who conceals his presence in prayer will have a penchant for drawing us to unseen, hidden actions outside prayer as a favorite way to please him.

~

God can be a beggar in rags as much as the transcendent mystery of Divine Persons. Sometimes it is good to recall that he exchanges one truth for another on the same day, even in the same hour of prayer.

~

A thirst for God in solitary prayer demands an expression of love in concrete actions, and that truth is readily accepted. But not so easily realized is that our actions tend to be shallow in love and largely exteriorized unless prior to them a thirst to love has been resolute in silent prayer alone with God.

～

It might be said that the concealment of silence modulates the tones of the divine voice in prayer as much as the habit of hiding determines the appearance of God when he is showing his face outside prayer.

～

What premonition of our own impoverishment at death hovers in the vicinity any time we venture closer to a poor man's life? But this may be a reason why we sometimes keep a safe distance from the poor.

～

It might be a fruitful grace to imagine that the priest and the scribe who walked past the man bloody and left for dead by robbers on the road to Jericho encountered another injured man on their return trip.

～

A soul may find itself in prayer peacefully affirming its commitment to God when unknown to it the cost of fidelity is soon to extend beyond everything it previously considered.

～

There is a spiritual drama implicit in all prayerful silence—our soul prostrate before a still undetermined future that must be embraced blindly, fearlessly, trusting in God and his kindness.

～

After a certain length of time together between those who love, an avowal of esteem becomes unnecessary. The permanence of friendship is understood on both sides. So, too, in our soul's friendship with God, we ought not to demand that he somehow prove his faithfulness. This can be trusted with certainty.

～

It may be much more the still painful poverty of our soul that draws divine love during an hour of prayer rather than, as we may surmise, an easy confidence of being loved by God.

～

The realization of being loved by God may come more often outside a time of prayer, not so readily within it. On the other hand, to make this desire to know and feel ourselves loved a primary aspiration of prayer would be a mistake. It cannot sustain a lifetime of prayer, nor a lifetime of effort in charity.

~

When a soul no longer has to understand the reasons behind God's requests, but is simply a servant to them, it is manifesting a fruit of a deeper commitment to prayer.

~

"My desire for God seems to have made my soul dissatisfied with everything that used to provide diversion to it." Such a person may be at the beginning of greater graces in prayer. But perhaps it is best to ask whether that same person would lay down an hour of prayer for the need of another person.

~

A desire for more time with God in prayer is inevitable when a soul is first drawn by God to solitary prayer. But it may initially bring as well a certain new uneasiness and discontent in the company of others. When a desire for God is behind this, who would forsake the one to limit the discomfort felt in the other?

~

We may feel in prayer that nothing is more desirable than to give ourselves entirely to God, even if it means costly suffering. Then we discover later in the day that what God especially wants is a small sacrifice we have been neglecting until this point.

~

The diminishment of sensitivity to ourselves outside prayer is a fruit of deeper prayer. When silent prayer is finished and we keep our eyes away from self, it is a sign we realize better we are never alone, a truth discovered first in silent prayer.

~

A tendency to self-effacement is characteristic of contemplatives. If there is a wish, on the contrary, to be recognized and lauded, any initial desire felt for deeper prayer will be like listening to a foreign language for the first time, perhaps sonorous in its tones, but impossible to understand.

~

There are no mirrors in heaven—nor, for that matter, in the possession of those who love God with intensity in this life.

∼

The yearning to disappear from our own thoughts in prayer is always to some degree in proportion to our soul's deeper longing for God.

∼

"Who am I that you should come to me? . . ." (Lk 1:43) This question of Saint Elizabeth to Mary ought to rise up within our heart whenever we experience a hunger for silent prayer.

∼

A sign that our soul may be drawing closer to God is to realize that while we may be more content than ever in our life, we have also become more incapable of a permanent satisfaction in anything this life can offer.

∼

There is an aspect of faith to which we do not pay sufficient attention. And this is that God may turn a poor man's face toward us one day to deliver his most earnest request to our lives.

∽

The hour in Nazareth when Mary declares her Fiat, "let it be done according to your word", is already, in the eternal mind of God, the hour in which the echo of these words reaches its crescendo in the crucifixion of her son at Calvary (Lk 1:38).

∽

"Let those, then, who are singularly active, who think they can win the world with their preaching and exterior works, observe here that they would profit the Church and please God much more, not to mention the good example they would give, were they to spend at least half of this time with God in prayer. . . . Without prayer, they would do a great deal of hammering but accomplish little, and sometimes nothing, and even at times cause harm. God forbid that the salt should begin to lose its savor (Mt 5:13), for however much they may appear to achieve externally, they will in substance be accomplishing nothing; it is beyond doubt that good works can be performed only by the power of God."

—Saint John of the Cross,
The Spiritual Canticle 29.3